KWYA

S0-AHA-432

The 20th Century's
MOST INFLUENTIAL
HISPANICS

Dolores Huerta
Labor Leader

by Debra A. Miller

LUCENT BOOKS
An imprint of Thomson Gale, a part of The Thomson Corporation

THOMSON
GALE

Detroit • New York • San Francisco • New Haven, Conn. • Waterville, Maine • London

THOMSON

GALE

LIBRARY OF CONGRESS CATALOGING-IN-PUBLICATION DATA

Miller, Debra A.
Dolores Huerta : labor leader / by Debra A. Miller.
   p. cm. — (Twentieth century's most influential hispanics)
Includes bibliographical references and index.
ISBN-13: 978-1-59018-971-9 (hard cover : alk. paper)
ISBN-10: 1-59018-971-X (hard cover : alk. paper)
1. Huerta, Dolores, 1930—Juvenile literature. 2. Women labor leaders—Juvenile literature—United States—Biography 3. Mexican American migrant agricultural laborers—Biography—Juvenile literature. 4. United Farm Workers—History—Juvenile literature. I. Title. II. Series.
HD6509.H84M55 2006
331.4'7813092—dc22
[B]
                                                              2006012604

Table of Contents

Foreword

When Alberto Gonzales was a boy living in Texas, he never dreamed he would one day stand next to the president of the United States. Born to poor migrant workers, Gonzales grew up in a two-bedroom house shared by his family of ten. There was no telephone or hot water. Because his parents were too poor to send him to college, Gonzales joined the Air Force, but after two years obtained an appointment to the Air Force Academy and, from there, transferred to Rice University. College was still a time of struggle for Gonzales, who had to sell refreshments in the bleachers during football games to support himself. But he eventually went on to Harvard Law School and rose to prominence in the Texas government. And then one day, decades after rising from his humble beginnings in Texas, he found himself standing next to President George W. Bush at the White House. The president had nominated him to be the nation's first Hispanic attorney general. As he accepted the nomination, Gonzales embraced the president and said, "'Just give me a chance to prove myself'—that is a common prayer for those in my community. Mr. President, thank you for that chance."

Like Gonzales, many Hispanics in America and elsewhere have shed humble beginnings to soar to impressive and previously unreachable heights. In the twenty-first century, influential Hispanic figures can be found worldwide and in all fields of endeavor including science, politics, education, the arts, sports, religion, and literature. Some accomplishments, like those of musician Carlos Santana or author Alisa Valdes-Rodriguez, have added a much-needed Hispanic voice to the artistic landscape. Others, such as revolutionary Che Guevara or labor leader Dolores Huerta, have spawned international social movements that have enriched the rights of all peoples.

But who exactly is Hispanic? When studying influential Hispanics, it is important to understand what the term actually

4

means. Unlike strictly racial categories like "black" or "Asian," the term "Hispanic" joins a huge swath of people from different countries, religions, and races. The category was first used by the U.S. census bureau in 1980 and is used to refer to Spanish-speaking people of any race. Officially, it denotes a person whose ancestry either descends in whole or in part from the people of Spain or from the various peoples of Spanish-speaking Latin America. Often the term "Hispanic" is used synonymously with the term "Latino," but the two actually have slightly different meanings. "Latino" refers to people only from the countries of Latin America, such as Argentina, Brazil, and Venezuela, whether they speak Spanish or Portuguese. Meanwhile, Hispanic refers to only Spanish-speaking peoples but from any Spanish-speaking country, such as Spain, Puerto Rico, or Mexico.

In America, Hispanics are reaching new heights of cultural influence, buying power, and political clout. More than 35 million people identified themselves as Hispanic on the 2000 U.S. census, and there were estimated to be more than 41 million Hispanics in America as of 2006. In the twenty-first century people of Hispanic origin have officially become the nation's largest ethnic minority, outnumbering both blacks and Asians. Hispanics constitute about 13 percent of the nation's total population, and by 2050 their numbers are expected to rise to 102.6 million, at which point they would account for 24 percent of the total population. With growing numbers and expanding influence, Hispanic leaders, artists, politicians, and scientists in America and in other countries are commanding attention like never before.

These unique and fascinating stories are the subjects of *The Twentieth Century's Most Influential Hispanics* collection from Lucent Books. Each volume in the series critically examines the challenges, accomplishments, and legacy of influential Hispanic figures; many of whom, like Alberto Gonzales, sprang from modest beginnings to achieve groundbreaking goals. *The Twentieth Century's Most Influential Hispanics* offers vivid narrative, fully documented primary and secondary source quotes, a bibliography, thorough index, and mix of color and black and white photographs which enhance each volume and provide excellent starting points for research and discussion.

A Passion for Justice

For more than half a century, Dolores Huerta has been fighting to improve the lives of Mexican Americans in the United States. In 1962, together with Cesar Chavez, she founded the predecessor to the United Farm Workers (UFW), the first successful union for some of the most powerless and exploited people in the country—the workers who pick most of the fruits and vegetables that end up on American tables. While Chavez became the public face of the union, Huerta worked behind the scenes performing multiple roles as chief labor organizer, contract negotiator, legislative lobbyist, and union strategist. Her enduring dedication to farmworkers, Latinos, women, and the poor have made her a role model not only within the Mexican American community but also for all people who want to make the world a better place.

The Work of the UFW

By creating the first union for farmworkers, Huerta and Chavez accomplished what many people considered an impossible task. Whereas farmers and growers were wealthy, well-connected politically, and powerful, most farm laborers were poor, desperate, uneducated Mexican Americans who often did not speak English and were afraid to assert themselves for fear of losing their jobs. Despite the daunting odds, and with no money or outside support, Huerta and Chavez built the UFW from the ground up through sheer hope, determination, and hard work. They persuaded lowly farmworkers to band together to demand change from their employers, using the usual union tools of strikes and picketing. They also implemented what are now recognized as novel and visionary strategies that brought the union national recognition and support. One of these strategies was the industry-wide consumer boycott—a technique in which the union publicized the problems and struggle of farmworkers and asked people across the country to stop buying nonunion produce, such as grapes and lettuce.

For more than half a century, Dolores Huerta has been fighting to improve the lives of Mexican Americans in the United States.

Using these methods, Huerta, Chavez, and the UFW placed economic pressure on growers until they agreed to work with the union. Over the years they successfully negotiated hundreds of contracts to protect the basic rights of farmworkers. Typical contract provisions provided for simple necessities, such as fresh drinking water and toilets for workers laboring in the hot, sun-baked fields, as well as significant wage and benefit increases, protections from pesticides, and other improvements in working conditions. Huerta and Chavez also helped workers by creating a farmworkers' credit union, medical plan, pension fund, housing agency, and radio station. Perhaps most importantly, by standing up for the poorest Latinos, the UFW provided all Latino Americans with a new sense of pride and hope. As Chavez once said, "The consciousness and pride that were raised by our union are alive and thriving inside millions of young Hispanics who will never work on a farm."[1]

Chavez died in 1993, but Huerta now carries on their joint vision for social change. Today she is a grandmother with eleven children, fifteen grandchildren, and four great-grandchildren. Yet she continues to help the UFW with organizing drives and speaks out frequently on issues important to farmworkers, Latinos, and others.

Huerta's Passion

To those who have known her, Huerta is both a heroine and an imperfect human. She is a tough, smart, outspoken, and confident leader; a loving mother; and a kindhearted and welcoming friend to many people. She has been criticized, however, for being an absent parent, for being a fiery and combative personality, and for frequent arguments with Chavez. Some commentators have described her as a "Mother Teresa [who] leads like General Patton."[2]

Yet her passionate nature may be her biggest strength. Known to farmworkers as La Pasionaria (the Passionate One), Huerta effectively used the force of her character and personality to her advantage in her work—to inspire workers, persuade legislators, and intimidate employers and their representatives at the bargaining table. As a public speaker, her dynamism and enthusiasm are irresistible; she often gets even sedate audiences up on their feet to support her cause and chant the UFW motto, *Sí se puede!* (Yes

Migrant worker camps such as this one from the 1950s offered the best living conditions that poorly paid farmworkers could hope to find.

it can be done!). Although she has been arrested twenty-two times (with no convictions), hospitalized twice for exhaustion caused by overwork, and severely beaten by police while protesting, she has continued to stand up for causes she believes in. Even now, almost nothing seems to slow her down.

Many writers have suggested that the key to Huerta's passion is her unwavering commitment to the ideals of justice and equality. As Chavez once said, "She just can't stand to see people pushed around."[3] She developed this sense of justice at an early age. As a girl, she was stung by the discrimination she witnessed against Latinos: She saw farmworkers who were unable to afford a place to live, and her own teachers did not believe she could write well because she was Mexican American. In adulthood, she tried other professions but could not ignore a compelling urge to work against the injustices she saw in American society. As a labor organizer and activist for farmworkers, she finally found her true calling.

Justice for All

Huerta, however, did not limit her activism to the role of a union organizer or Latino activist. She also has reached out to

A celebrity in her own right, the diminutive Huerta joined singer Bonnie Raitt (far left) and actor Danny Glover (left) in a 2003 peace march.

African Americans and others working for fairness and equality in society. Beginning in the 1970s, she became actively involved in women's rights, a cause that she continues to champion today. Huerta's vision of a just society has always encompassed everyone, regardless of race or gender.

To achieve positive social change, Huerta advocated that the powerless must take responsibility for themselves, join forces to gain strength, and then negotiate for their rightful share of America's bounty. Another key belief held strongly by both Chavez and Huerta is the importance of nonviolent struggle and advocacy. Like Mahatma Gandhi, the revered Indian leader who organized thousands of people to engage in nonviolent actions to force Britain out of colonial India, Chavez and Huerta knew that nonviolence gives protesters moral superiority and protects them from being dismissed by authorities as mere troublemakers.

Over the years Huerta's basic views have not changed. She continues to fight for what she thinks is right and good, and she is fearless and forceful in speaking her mind, whether talking to heads of state or high school students. She clearly has earned the many awards and tributes that have come her way in recent years, and she deserves a place of honor in the annals of American history.

Chapter 1

Lessons from Childhood

The lessons of Dolores Huerta's childhood, both positive and negative, strongly contributed to her career and achievements as a labor organizer and activist. The daughter of poor but proud Mexican American parents, she never lacked for the necessities of life and she was blessed with powerful role models in her ambitious father and her strong-willed, hardworking mother. Yet as a young Chicana (female Mexican American) who attended school with wealthier whites during an era of deeply entrenched racial segregation and inequality, Dolores also learned early lessons about discrimination, poverty, and injustice. Raised in a farming community where she had ample contact with poor, powerless migrant farmworkers, she eventually grew up to become their advocate.

Humble Beginnings

Dolores Clara Fernandez was born on April 10, 1930, in Dawson, a small coal-mining town high in the mountains of northern New Mexico. Today the mines have been closed and Dawson is a ghost town, but early in its history it was bustling and prosperous, with spacious homes, a modern hospital, schools, a movie theater, a department store, and various other businesses and amusements. Dolores's parents were Juan Fernandez, a young coal miner, and his wife, Alicia Chavez Fernandez. Both parents were of mixed Mexican and Spanish ancestry but were born in the United States. Her mother was a second-generation Mexican American; her father's parents had immigrated to America from Mexico just before he was born. Dolores was the second of the couple's three children and their only daughter. Dolores had two brothers, one older, John, and one younger, Marshall.

At the time of Dolores's birth, the country was in the midst of economic hard times. A catastrophic U.S. stock market crash in 1929 had plunged Americans and much of the world into the Great Depression, a period in which banks failed, businesses went bankrupt, investors lost their life savings, and millions of people lost their jobs. Many people even lost their homes and could not

Huerta's father, Juan Fernandez, worked in this coal mine in Dawson, New Mexico, at the time of her birth in 1930.

feed their families. Thousands of able-bodied men were reduced to standing in soup lines to receive handouts of free food to survive. These conditions lasted for close to ten years and were especially difficult for Mexican Americans and other minorities, who already represented a disproportionate share of the nation's poor or underprivileged.

The strain of trying to survive in the Depression economy soon affected the young Fernandez family. When Dolores was only three years old, her parents divorced, leaving her and her two brothers in the care of their mother. Alicia Fernandez then struggled to provide for her family as a single parent.

Early Life

The divorce separated Dolores from her father, and she lost almost all regular contact with him after he was fired from the mines and left Dawson to find work elsewhere. Like coal miners everywhere during the difficult Depression years, Juan Fernandez had to endure dirty, difficult, and dangerous working conditions for low pay. He believed, however, that the miners should have a say in how they were paid and about the conditions in which they had to work, and he tried to organize the workers to form a union. For this, Fernandez was fired; employers at this time controlled their workforce with little government supervision or restriction, and plenty of unemployed, uncomplaining men were willing to take his place. After he left mining, Fernandez became a migrant farmworker, harvesting beets across the country, in places as far away as Nebraska and Wyoming. As a farmworker, he worked long, backbreaking hours in the fields, earned very little, and had limited contact with his children.

In 1936, when Dolores was six, her mother moved the family to Stockton, a town in northern California about 60 miles (97km) east of San Francisco in the middle of the rich and fertile farmlands of California's Central Valley. Here, Alicia Fernandez worked two jobs—as a waitress during the day and in a canning factory at night—to make enough money to support the family. Alicia's father, Herculano Chavez, a disabled miner who could no longer work, helped out by caring for his grandchildren while their

Unemployed people wait in line for food during the Great Depression. The economic hardships of the times broke apart Huerta's family.

mother was working. He often entertained the youngsters with stories, and he provided patient supervision and affection to the intelligent and verbal young Dolores. She has said, "My grandfather used to call me seven tongues because I always talked so much."[4] Through this time together, Dolores became very close to her grandfather. Despite the financial pressures of the times, Dolores never lacked for food, shelter, or love, and she always remembered her early life with great fondness.

Growing Up

As Dolores entered her teenage years in the early 1940s, the U.S. economy rebounded and the Depression finally lifted, thanks largely to a boost in manufacturing and production created by World War II. The United States entered the war in December 1941, following the Japanese bombing of Pearl Harbor. The financial situation of Dolores's family also improved dramatically at this time, due in part to another aspect of the war. In May 1942, with the United States at war with Japan, the federal government ordered the forced relocation of some 120,000 Japanese Americans living on the West Coast, most of whom were U.S. citizens, to internment camps, where they stayed for the duration of the war. Among those ordered to move was a Japanese family who owned a seventy-room hotel and restaurant in a run-down part of Stockton, where Alicia Fernandez was employed. She purchased the property the family had to relinquish, as well as a second smaller hotel. Alicia proved herself a capable manager and good businessperson, and the hotels earned a tidy profit.

Also during this time, Alicia married a man named James Richards, and they had another child, giving Dolores and her brothers a half sister. The new family lived in one hotel, named the Richards Hotel, and everybody worked in the family business—renting and cleaning the rooms, serving guests, and keeping the books. Even Dolores and her siblings helped out at the hotel in the evenings, on weekends, and during school breaks. Alicia's independence and assertiveness, however, eventually caused her second

During World War II, Huerta's mother bought a hotel from Japanese Americans who were forced to go to an internment camp like this one.

marriage, like her first, to end in divorce. In the 1950s she was married a third time, to Juan Silva. According to all reports, this marriage was a contented one. It produced another half sister for Dolores and lasted until her mother's death.

Alicia's entrepreneurial success allowed young Dolores to enjoy a fairly typical middle-class American adolescence. With her mother's encouragement, she took violin, piano, and dance lessons, and she especially loved dancing. At one point she wanted to be a flamenco dancer when she grew up. During high school Dolores became a majorette and marched with the school band in many local parades. She participated in a number of other

Farmworkers wait to be taken to the fields in the 1940s in Stockton, California, where Huerta grew up.

extracurricular activities as well, such as singing in the church choir and joining the local Girl Scout troop. Dolores remained active in Girl Scouts until she graduated from high school, and through the organization she became involved in a number of community and fund-raising events. She also volunteered with church groups and other organizations, helping to organize activities for annual Mexican Independence Day fiestas and gathering donations of food for the poor. In addition, Dolores and her siblings often attended the symphony and theater to see live music performances of renowned artists, thanks to season tickets purchased by their mother.

Deeper Meaning

"In Spanish, the name Dolores means sorrow. Huerta means orchard. . . . The name foretold her life."

Bonnie Dahl, journalist. Bonnie Dahl, "Mission Dolores," *Prism Online*, October 1995. www.journalism.sfsu.edu/www/pubs/prism/oct95/mission.html.

Young Dolores, too, was a good student who loved to write poems and stories. A pretty girl, with dark eyes and long black hair, she had an outgoing personality and many friends. A former classmate from Stockton High School recalls, "When we were in school, [Dolores] was popular and outspoken. She was already an organizer, but I didn't think she'd get so serious and work for such a cause."[5]

Role Models

Besides providing Dolores with stability, financial security, and opportunities to pursue her many interests, her mother, Alicia, acted as an important role model for her daughter—an example of female strength, equality, and compassion that Dolores admired. Although she was a single parent much of the time, Alicia was a forceful personality who, through sheer grit, determination, and resourcefulness, managed to raise her children and provide them with a comfortable life. Alicia's success as a mother under these difficult conditions taught the children strong values of hard work, hope, and perseverance.

As a businesswoman during the 1940s and the 1950s, Alicia also broke the mold of the traditional Mexican wife and mother, and she was equally ambitious for her children. She encouraged both her sons and her daughters to get an education, to become involved with others in community activities, and to fully develop their talents and skills. Alicia also provided a home in which the children were not expected to conform to the traditional gender roles of Latino culture, in which the woman is expected to serve the man. Huerta explains, "My mother was a strong woman and she didn't favor my brothers. There was no idea that men were superior. At home, we all shared equally in the household tasks: I never had to cook for my brothers or do their clothes like in many traditional Mexican families."[6]

By her own example, Alicia also taught Dolores to be independent, self-confident, and unafraid to speak her mind. Huerta recalls, "My mother was . . . a business woman, she had a restau-

The Plight of Farmworkers

Life has always been difficult for the farmworkers who pick America's fruits and vegetables. Farmworkers labor in the hot sun for hours, often bending over or reaching up in awkward positions to pick delicate crops such as grapes, tomatoes, and strawberries. On many farms there are no toilets in the fields, no fresh drinking water, and no place to rest or take breaks. Also, the workers are frequently exposed to dangerous chemicals in fertilizers and pesticides used on the produce. Many workers live a migratory life, following the harvests from farm to farm. These workers are sometimes provided with run-down housing by growers, but otherwise they sleep in cheap rented rooms, in their cars, or outside on the ground.

For this demanding and dangerous work, farmworkers have historically been paid some of the lowest wages in the United States, often less than government poverty guidelines. In addition, many of California's farmworkers are Mexicans or Mexican Americans who know little English and lack education. These conditions made farmworkers one of the most exploited and powerless groups of workers in the country and the most difficult to organize for union activities.

rant and hotels, she owned a business. So that was my role model growing up."[7] Another time, Huerta said, "My mother was one of those women who do a lot. She was divorced, so I never really understood what it was like to take a back seat to a man."[8]

Alicia Arong, Dolores's younger half sister, paints a similar picture of their mother, explaining, "Mom was a women's libber before her time. She felt very strongly that women should get out and work and participate in the community."[9] Indeed, Alicia proved to be adept at community service and organizing. At one point she won first prize in Stockton for a community voter-registration drive.

Many observers say this example of feminism and egalitarian family life was instrumental in giving Huerta a strong sense of self, inner strength, and assertiveness—qualities that later helped her to become a great leader. Writer Ruth Carranza explains, "For Huerta there was no sexual discrimination in her home and consequently no sense of inferiority or no encouragement to accept a sense of secondary role in her life and later in her work with the union. Also, there [were] no contradictory masculine/feminine messages by her mother."[10]

In addition, Dolores's mother actively participated in and exposed her children to a multicultural, multiracial community during an era of widespread racial segregation in the United States. The part of Stockton where the family lived was a poor neighborhood that was home to people of many different races and ethnic groups. Dolores grew up surrounded by Chinese, Latino, Native American, Italian, African American, Jewish, and Japanese families. She was taught that racial and ethnic equality was normal and appropriate. "We were all rather poor," Huerta states, "but it was an integrated community so it was not racist for me in my childhood."[11]

Even Dolores's Girl Scout troop was unique. The troop was made up of girls from diverse ethnic backgrounds, including African American, Chinese, Filipino, and Latino. This diversity helped Dolores to be comfortable around all people, including whites. She recalls, "All the Chicanos who went to school where I did are all making it. We grew up in Stockton, but weren't in a ghetto. As a result, we didn't have a whole bunch of hang-ups like hating Anglos [whites], or hating Blacks."[12]

Because the hotels the family owned catered to farmworkers, Dolores also gained valuable insight into the workers' struggles and difficult lives and developed a compassionate interest in their welfare. As her half sister Arong puts it, "We saw a lot of life out our windows."[13] Dolores learned, for example, that hard work in the fields usually paid very little and often left farmworkers without enough money to pay for even the most basic necessities, such as food and housing. Sometimes Dolores's mother let farmworkers and their families stay in her hotels for free if they could not afford to pay. Other times farmworkers paid for their rooms with fruits and vegetables that their employers let them take home. Dolores even experienced farmwork herself; during school vacations she spent some time working in an apricot-processing plant, where she stood all day and performed the repetitive task of cutting the apricots in half with a sharp knife.

Dolores stayed in touch as much as she could with her father as she was growing up and heard from him, too, about his expe-

In a common scene from the 1940s and 1950s, migrant farmworkers sleep on a warehouse platform rather than stay in the dismal camps provided for them.

riences with the terrible working conditions and injustices endured by farmworkers. Juan Fernandez was ambitious, however, and his interest in labor organizing led him to leave farmwork, earn a college degree, and become secretary-treasurer of the local union at the American Metals Company in New Mexico. In 1938 he was even elected to the New Mexico state legislature, where he devoted himself to improving labor laws. Although he was absent from her life much of the time, Dolores was proud of her father's education, commitment to union ideals, and accomplishments. He, like her mother, provided a living example of personal pride, perseverance, and achievement against difficult odds.

Experiences with Discrimination

Despite the many positive influences on her early life, Dolores was not completely insulated from society's darker side. In high school she experienced firsthand the poverty, discrimination, and segregation suffered by Mexican Americans in those days. Similar problems still afflict society today, but in the 1940s racism and prejudice were even worse because there were no laws prohibiting discrimination. On many occasions Huerta has reflected on this period of her life. She states, "[My high school was] pretty racist . . . [with] a big division between a lot of the rich kids from the north side and the poor kids from the south side and east side. There was a lot of discrimination . . . so it was a struggle to get through high school because of the racism in the school."[14] Huerta also has said that the "constant discrimination against . . . Latinos" that she experienced in her teenage years "crushed" her.[15]

Huerta has described several instances when she personally faced discrimination. One time, for example, the teenage Dolores entered an annual national Girl Scout essay contest and won second prize, which was a trip to the Hopi Indian Reservation in Gallup, New Mexico. When she asked for time off from school to go on the trip, however, she was denied by the dean of girls, even though her teachers supported her request and many white girls had previously been given time off for winning the same award. Dolores believed she was not permitted to go on the trip because she was the first Chicana ever to win the prize. She also lost out on another prize in a student contest to sell war bonds.

She won the contest by selling the most bonds, but she was never given the prize. Again, she attributed this discrimination to her being a Mexican American.

On another occasion during her senior year of high school, Dolores was given a final grade of "C" in her English class even though she had received numerous "A" grades on term papers, essays, and reports throughout the year. When she questioned her teacher about the low grade, the teacher explained that she had lowered Dolores's grade because her essays and reports were so good that she did not believe that Dolores had written them herself. Like other slights she had experienced, Dolores attributed this to the fact that she was Mexican American. She says, "That really discouraged me because I used to stay up all night and think, and try to make every paper different, and try to put words in there that I thought were nice."[16]

Dolores sometimes protested these injustices at school. Once, for example, she was a member of a school club that was planning a school dance. When other club members wanted to charge students three dollars to get into the event, Dolores quit the club in protest because she knew that many poor Mexican American students could not afford to pay what was then a large amount of money just to go to a dance.

An Unlikely Leader

"No one imagined that she would have gone on to lead the grand movement."

Lyrics from "Corrido de Dolores Huerta," ballad written about Dolores Huerta. Quoted in Margaret Rose, "Dolores Huerta: Passionate Defender of La Causa." http://chavez.cde.ca.gov/ModelCurriculum/Teachers/Lessons/Resources/Documents/Dolores_Huerta_Essay.pdf.

Huerta also remembers an incident involving a storefront owned by a friend of her mother's, where she and her friends used to congregate and practice a popular dance called the jitterbug. Dolores had persuaded local businessmen to donate a jukebox and a Ping-Pong table to give the teenagers somewhere to go and something to do after school. The police shut the place down, however. Huerta explains, "[The police] told us they didn't want to see all those white kids playing around with all these niggers, Filipinos and

Mexicans."[17] In yet another incident, on VJ (Victory over Japan) Day, the day World War II ended, her brother Marshall dressed up in a colorful outfit and went out to join the town's celebrations. Dolores and a friend planned to meet him at a dance, but on the way there they found Marshall badly beaten, with his new clothes torn to shreds. The beating was a racially motivated attack because he was a Mexican American dressed in flashy new clothes.

As a result of these types of experiences, Dolores began to understand the widespread inequalities between rich and poor and between whites and other ethnicities and races in American society. The unfairness and injustice of these realities became even clearer at age seventeen, when Dolores's mother took her on a trip to visit Mexico City. There, Dolores saw a culture in which people of Hispanic/Latino ancestry were the majority and were not treated badly, as they were in the United States. "This trip," Huerta

America in Transition

The 1940s through the 1960s, when Dolores Huerta was growing up and entering adulthood, were tumultuous times for the United States. The 1940s were dominated by World War II, a conflict that required many young men to enter the armed forces as soldiers. The manpower shortages created by the war allowed many women to enter the workforce for the first time, working in factories to help the war effort. This period was also a time when racial segregation was widespread and mandated by law. Many states required African Americans, Latino Americans, Native Americans, and Asian Americans to be segregated from whites in school, at work, and in their neighborhoods.

When the war ended in 1945, women gave up their jobs to returning soldiers, and nonwhite veterans were expected to return to their traditional place in society. Experiences in less discriminatory parts of the world, however, caused African Americans and others to begin a struggle for greater freedoms at home. A civil rights movement in the 1950s and the 1960s, featuring numerous street marches and protests, eventually led to an end to legal segregation, laws against racial discrimination in employment and housing, and improvements in the lives of many nonwhite citizens.

Throngs gather in Mexico City's central plaza. Huerta's visit to the city as a teen gave her a new perspective on being Mexican American.

recalls, "opened my eyes to that fact that there was nothing wrong with Chicanos."[18] She returned from Mexico motivated to do her best to help poor Mexican families in the United States. She joined Hispanic women's groups, such as the Comité Honorífico Women's Club, hoping these would provide a path of meaningful service. She quickly tired of these groups, however, because they mostly held dances and similar social functions and did not seem to be making a real difference in the world.

Dolores graduated from Stockton High School in 1947. She has said, "Most of the Latino kids that I graduated grammar school with dropped out of high school . . . [but] it would've never occurred to me to even think about dropping out. My parents both had a high school education."[19] Still, she was unsure of exactly what she would do with her life. She enrolled in the University of the Pacific in Stockton, planning on a teaching career. Her early life had given her a compassionate heart, an agile mind, and a strong sense of self; with these tools for success, she was now ready to enter the adult world. Guiding her were her mother's constant instructions while growing up—to follow her heart, trust her own strength, and "be yourself." This advice became her lifelong creed.

Chapter 2

Mother and Social Activist

Like her mother, Dolores Huerta embarked on an adult life that included several marriages and many children as well as full-time work. Although she loved her children and family life, Huerta discovered that her true passion was fighting injustice through social activism. She made this choice at a young age, but it soon became the first step in a lifetime career as an activist—a career that tested her personal relationships and constantly challenged her ability to provide and care for her growing family.

A Young Wife, Mother, and Student

Following her graduation from high school, Huerta attended college classes in Stockton at the University of the Pacific (now called San Joaquin Delta College). After two years, however, at age nineteen, she dropped out to marry Ralph Head, her high school sweetheart. At age twenty Huerta gave birth to her first child, a girl named Celeste. The young couple soon had another daughter, Lori, but the young parents proved to be incompatible and the marriage quickly ended in divorce. After the divorce, while her mother took care of her two girls, Huerta tried several different jobs. She worked for a time managing a grocery store, as a secretary in a naval supply base, and then in a sheriff's office.

Huerta was unhappy in all of these jobs, however, and decided to return to school. Yet even school did not satisfy her because she felt so frustrated about the injustices she saw in the society around her. She has written, "I felt I had all of these frustrations inside me. I had a fantastic complex because I seemed to be out of step with everybody and everything. You're trying to go to school and yet you see all of these injustices. It was just such a complex."[20] In 1955 Dolores graduated from college with a teaching certificate, the first child in her family to earn a higher education. This accomplishment was remarkable for that time in history, when most women, even whites, did not attend college or receive any education past the high school level.

After graduating from college Dolores taught elementary school for a short time in an area where most of her students

Children get water from an irrigation ditch near the migrant camp where they lived in the 1950s.

were the sons and daughters of poor Mexican American farm-workers. Yet she quickly tired of this work, even though she was helping children, she felt she was still not doing enough to serve others. She has said, "I couldn't stand seeing farm worker children come to class hungry and in need of shoes. I thought I could do more by organizing their parents than by trying to teach their hungry children."[21]

Finding Her Calling

Later in 1955 Huerta finally found what she had been looking for—the chance to actively work to help the poor and the powerless. This life-altering moment in Huerta's life came when she met a community activist named Fred Ross, who had traveled to Stockton to form a chapter of the Community Service Organization (CSO), a grassroots group he had founded a few years earlier in Los Angeles. The CSO was dedicated to fighting for reforms to help poor Mexican Americans in California. The bilingual news service *La Voz de Aztlan* explains: "The CSO battled segregation and police brutality, led voter registration drives, pushed for improved public services and fought to enact new legislation."[22] The CSO's approach to activism was one that appealed to Huerta; it involved poor people in community organizing and then taught them how to fight for improvements themselves.

Huerta attended one of Ross's talks for potential volunteers in Stockton. In Los Angeles, Ross explained, the CSO had improved the way the police treated Mexican Americans and had succeeded in getting a health clinic built for the poor. At this first meeting, Ross immediately recognized Huerta as someone who had the intelligence, passion, and determination to launch the Stockton CSO office. Newspaper editor and author Jacques E. Levy describes the young woman at this stage of her life: "Although twenty-five, . . . Huerta looked more like a teenager than a mother of two toddlers. She was small, slender, with striking Indian features and long, shiny black hair. Her tongue moved as swiftly as her mind, and both left most other mortals in their wake."[23]

Huerta, however, was skeptical about the CSO at first. Although impressed by Ross's achievements and approach, she worried that he might be involved in social work merely to advance the political philosophy of communism, which was then embraced by leaders of the Soviet Union, a U.S. enemy. Because of her previous work in a sheriff's office, Huerta knew how to look into Ross's background. She explains, "I thought Fred Ross from the Community Service Organization . . . was a Communist, so I went to the FBI [Federal Bureau of Investigation] and had him checked out. I really did that."[24]

Reaching the Top

"It is not easy for Latino men to have a woman as leader. [Huerta] has not only had to earn her way, but fight her way. Her competence, commitment and intelligence frighten a lot of people."

Lori de Leon, Huerta's daughter. Quoted in Bonnie Dahl, "Mission Dolores," *Prism Online*, October 1995. www.journalism.sfsu.edu/www/pubs/prism/oct95/mission.html.

Realizing that Ross was truly committed to improving the plight of the poor, Huerta ultimately decided to volunteer her time to help found the Stockton chapter of the CSO. She felt that she had finally found her calling. "This was, of course, something I had been looking for all my life," she later said. "I just felt like I had found a pot of gold!"[25]

Huerta credits her meeting with Ross as the key event that led her into a career as an activist and organizer. "If I hadn't met Fred Ross then, I don't know if I ever would have been organizing," she has said.

> People don't realize their own worth, and I wouldn't have realized what I could do unless someone had shown faith in me. At that time we were organizing against racial discrimination—the way Chicanos were treated by the police, courts, politicians. I had taken the status quo for granted. But Fred said it could change. So I started working.[26]

Huerta spent the next several years juggling her job as a teacher with her new avocation as an activist for the CSO. In making the fateful choice to become an activist and labor organizer, she committed herself to a life of hard work, constant travel, and near poverty. Activists, especially in those days, did not earn much money and were kept very busy because of the enormous challenges of fighting for social change.

The Community Service Organization

The Community Service Organization (CSO) was founded by activist Fred Ross in 1949 in response to widespread police abuse and discrimination against Mexican Americans in California. The CSO became a leader in the Latino struggle for equality and justice and helped to train many early Latino leaders, including Dolores Huerta, in community organizing techniques.

Fred Ross was a student and admirer of the ideas of Saul Alinsky, a Chicago activist who, in 1940, started a network of grassroots activist offices focused on specific social and political goals, such as improving wages. Alinsky favored nonviolent confrontations with authorities to create conflict and draw attention to social causes. He is often credited with laying the foundation for the civil rights movement of the 1950s and the confrontational politics of the 1960s. Ross put Alinsky's tactics into practice to organize poor Mexican Americans in California and teach them to fight against police brutality and for better education, housing, and jobs. The main thrust of Ross's vision, which Dolores Huerta shared, was to help the poor take an active role in fighting for and demanding their fair share of society's wealth.

Chicago activist Saul Alinsky favored nonviolent action.

Huerta's Achievements with the CSO

In the early days of her CSO work, Huerta focused on fund-raising, conducting registration drives to get more Mexican Americans to vote, and pushing local government agencies to provide services to Mexican Americans. Impressed by her skills and dedication, however, the CSO soon hired her to lobby the California state government in Sacramento for legal reforms that would benefit poor Latinos. In mid-twentieth-century America, this was a very untraditional job for a young Latina. The Dolores Huerta Foundation's Web site explains: "She became a fearless lobbyist in Sacramento, at . . . a time when few women, not to mention women of color, dared to enter the State Capital and National Capital to lobby legislators."[27]

Despite the obstacles, however, Huerta loved her job and was very successful. She was a natural leader, who had no sense of inferiority despite her race or her gender. Women were generally not taken seriously by most men at this point in American history, but Huerta was not intimidated in the least by men, even when they held positions of power in the legislature or elsewhere. Indeed, the CSO job seemed tailor-made for the young Huerta because it provided her with the chance to finally use her skills and enthusiasm to serve the poor and make a difference in the world—challenges that gave her great personal satisfaction and self-esteem. She explains: "I like social change. I feel humble because I've been very fortunate in my life. God has put me in the position and provided the opportunities and skills to get things done."[28]

During the years she worked with the CSO, Huerta helped to pass fifteen bills. In 1960, for example, her efforts were key in passing legislation giving Spanish speakers the right to take driver's license exams in their native language. In 1961 she successfully lobbied for landmark legislation that allowed Mexican workers who had legally entered the United States and were residents of California to receive old-age security pensions and state disability insurance. Before then, such workers were denied these government benefits because, although they were legal residents, they were not U.S. citizens. In 1963 she was instrumental in acquiring federal welfare benefits, under the Aid to Families with

Dependent Children program, for unemployed and underemployed farmworkers and their families. She also helped to pass a law that provides Spanish-speaking voters in California with ballots in the Spanish language.

In another CSO campaign, in 1962, Huerta traveled to Washington, D.C., to push federal legislators to end the bracero program, which was started in 1941. This program allowed Mexican laborers to immigrate to the United States to temporarily work in agriculture due to a shortage of American workers during World War II. The bracero program helped American farmers make large profits, but it was considered legalized slavery by many critics because of its exploitation of Mexican workers, who were paid extremely low wages and were required to work long

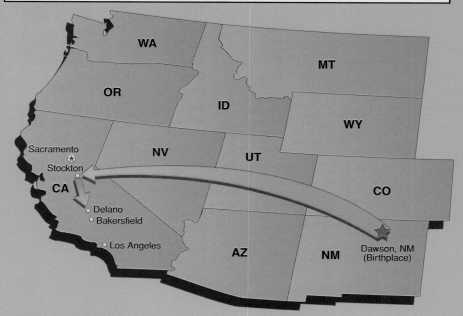

Map of the Early Life of Dolores Huerta

In 1930 Dolores Huerta was born in the small mining town of Dawson, New Mexico. When she was six, her mother moved the family to Stockton, California, the place Dolores would live until 1962. When Cesar Chavez offered her a job with the newly founded National Farm Workers Association, she moved to Delano, California. This small city would set the national stage for a movement that would eventually envelope the whole country.

Mexican nationals cross the border to work on U.S. farms under the bracero program.

hours under horrible conditions. Despite the criticism and efforts to defeat it, however, the bracero operation was not officially terminated by Congress until 1964.

Family Life

Huerta's work for the CSO during this period also brought her into contact with her second husband. Early in her tenure at the organization, she met and married Ventura Huerta, a CSO coworker. The marriage quickly produced five children: Fidel, Emilio, Vincent, Alicia, and Angela. Including her two girls from her first marriage, Celeste and Lori, Huerta now had a family of seven children. Despite her growing family and deepening domestic responsibilities, she continued to work as an activist and lobbyist, often traveling away from home for long periods of time, even when she was pregnant.

Huerta's strong personality and dedication to her work for the CSO eventually destroyed her marriage to Ventura. Her assertive style may have been one problem. When she first became involved in organizing farmworkers while with the CSO, Dolores even reportedly forced Ventura to quit his job and work with her; she needed a man to act as a "front" person after her priest pressured her not to do the work herself because he thought that labor organizing was no job for a woman. Her activist work also made things difficult for the family financially. She has explained, "It was difficult for us . . . to work for nothing, because I was having a baby every year. They were hard times!"[29]

Ventura also frequently objected that her family always seemed to come second to her work. He wanted her to scale back her work and community involvements and spend more time at home with him and the children. These were demands, however, that Dolores could not fulfill. Her daughter Juanita Chavez has said, "It was difficult for them [her husbands] with the life she chose to lead. Her marriage has been to her work."[30] Huerta herself has admitted that some of the most difficult times of her life were when she was married. "Just having to live in the role of an oppressed woman," she says, "I found very difficult."[31]

The Organizer
"She'll probably die organizing."

Fidel Huerta, Dolores Huerta's son. Quoted in Bonnie Dahl, "Mission Dolores," *Prism Online*, October 1995. www.journalism.sfsu.edu/www/pubs/prism/oct95/mission.html.

After years of conflict, Dolores and Ventura separated and then divorced, but Dolores kept the name Huerta. She later described their breakup: "When I remember the day I broke up with Mr. Huerta, it was horrible. We had this big fight at 5 o'clock in the morning, and the next day I had this big meeting that I had organized in Contra Costa County. I didn't sleep all night and I just got in the car to go to the meeting."[32] The divorce from Ventura was not amicable; the couple fought bitterly over custody of their five children. In the end, Dolores was awarded custody of all the children except for the oldest boy, Fidel, who went to live with his father for several years. Later, even Fidel returned to live with his mother. Huerta was once again a single mother, this time responsible for seven young children. She continued working as hard as ever, however, and her mother stepped in to help as she had in

The Bracero Program

Bracero workers pick chili peppers in 1964.

In 1942 the United States and Mexico agreed to implement the Bracero Program, a legislative scheme that permitted Mexican citizens to legally migrate to the United States to obtain temporary agricultural work. The program came about because of a labor shortage in the United States caused by so many men leaving the country to fight in World War II. Even after the war, however, the program continued. During its twenty-two-year life, the Bracero Program brought more than 4.5 million Mexican workers into the country, many to California and Texas. Most were Mexican peasants who were desperate for work and were willing to accept very low wages. Under the agreement between the United States and Mexico, braceros were supposed to receive certain protections, such as housing, medical treatment, transportation, and wages equal to those of American farmworkers, but these provisions were often ignored by American employers. After much criticism, the Bracero Program was finally terminated in 1964.

the past. Friends and coworkers also often pitched in to take care of her children.

According to most reports, Huerta never officially married again, but she did have a long-term relationship with Richard Chavez, the brother of Cesar Chavez. The two met and became close in the early 1970s after Huerta became involved with union work, and they had four children together—Juanita, Maria Elena, Ricky, and Camilla. This enlarged her already large brood to eleven children; the last child was born when she was forty-six years old. In Richard Chavez, Huerta finally found a man who shared her passion for social change. Of all her romantic relationships, this one proved to be the most stable and enduring, lasting for decades into the present.

Tensions Between Motherhood and Career

In addition to placing great strain on her marriages and relationships, Huerta's single-minded dedication to her work also created a lifelong tension with her role as a mother and provider. Huerta acknowledges that her choice of careers meant that she was away from her children often, sometimes even as long as three or four months at a time. She has admitted: "The time I spend with my kids is very limited."[33] Over the years Huerta missed countless school events, holidays, and birthdays that were important to her children. Whenever she could, she took them with her—on picket lines, on organizing visits, and even on trips to more glamorous places such as New York. Sometimes, however, when she was traveling, the children had to be split up to stay in the homes of different family members or friends. These separations were necessary to allow Huerta to do her work, but they disrupted the children's routines and undermined their sense of home and security.

Because of Huerta's sparse income, sometimes as low as five to thirty-five dollars per week, the family also had to live mostly on donated food and clothing. Huerta's children often had to face their peers at school wearing tattered clothing, and they lacked the toys and material goods that their school friends took for granted. As Huerta said in a 1998 interview, "Like most working women, you have these guilt complexes, especially in my case because we lived in poverty and my kids didn't have the proper care they needed. But when people ask, 'How could you do it?' Well, you do it without thinking about it, because if you think about it, you can't do it."[34]

Even worse, Huerta's children had to deal with the reality that they were less important to her than her work. In both her actions and words, Huerta left no doubt that she was committed, first and foremost, to promoting social change. Lori de Leon, Huerta's second-oldest daughter, for example, tells a story about a time when she was about to turn thirteen:

> My mother was going to Florida [on a business trip]. . . . I was upset; it was going to be my birthday. I was at the office and I said, "We don't even see you, my birthday is coming, why can't you be with me?" My mother said, "Your birthday is important, I understand what you are saying. But you have to understand there are thousands and thousands of farm worker children out there who don't get to celebrate their birthdays. You can help me by sacrificing your birthday." I never forgot this. All of us knew that the work was more important.[35]

Huerta faced heavy criticism for her neglect of her children, even from family and friends. In a 1974 interview, she said,

> I had a lot of doubts to begin with, but I had to act in spite of my conflict between my family and my commitment [to my work]. My biggest problem was not to feel guilty about it. I don't any more, but then, everybody used to lay these guilt trips on me, about what a bad mother I was, neglecting my children. My own relatives were the hardest, especially when my kids were small; you know, they were stair steps—I had six and one on the way when I started—and I was driving around Stockton with all these little babies in the car, the different diaper changes for each one.[36]

On the other hand, according to most accounts, Huerta's children always knew they were loved by their mother. De Leon has related, "It never fails to amaze me that each time I was in the hospital having a baby . . . and I was there lying on the table and my mom's supposed to be 2,000 or 3,000 miles away, she shows up at the foot of the bed saying, 'O.K., push.'"[37] And her daughter Juanita Chavez, calls her simply "my hero."[38]

Huerta also says the children, through their experiences growing up in her household, learned important lessons about social responsibility, relating to other people, and the insignificance of material goods. Huerta says,

> I can look back and say it's O.K. because my kids turned out fine, even though at times they had to fend for themselves, other people took care of them, and so on. . . . Taking my kids all over the states made them lose their fear of people, of new situations. . . . My kids are totally politicized mentally and the whole

Huerta greets children during a Democratic Party campaign. She spent little time with her own children while working on farmerworker issues.

idea of working without material gain has made a great difference in the way they think.[39]

Huerta even tells of an incident in which one of her daughters turned down a friend's offer to buy her brand new clothes in New York City; the girl came home with only a couple of items because she felt that a splurge on fancy new clothes would be too materialistic.

Huerta, too, instilled the same egalitarian values in her own children that her mother had taught her. "My kids grew up where the girls did not have to do for their brothers," she says. "My sons had to do it for themselves because I was gone so much of the time, you know. They had the privilege to take care of themselves and to be resourceful."[40] Today Huerta's children are all successful. Among them are an attorney, a paralegal, a chef, a therapist, a performance artist, an administrator, and a medical doctor. In a recent interview, Huerta confided, "Now that I've seen how good [my children] turned out, I don't feel so guilty."[41]

The truth of Huerta's life, therefore, is that she juggled her two roles of mother and activist as best she could while staying true to her dream of promoting social change. Although some critics would say that she sacrificed her family for her work, others believe she did both jobs well. A reflection by Unitarian minister and ethicist Jone Johnson Lewis about Huerta supports this view:

> I always think of Dolores Huerta with another image in addition to her crucial role in labor history. In 1976, I attended a dinner where she was to be honored for her contributions to social change. My older son was only a few months old at the time, and during one part of the evening, I left the main room to nurse him. I found myself next to Huerta, also nursing one of her children, and we exchanged typical new-mother oohs and aaahs over each other's children and spoke briefly of issues of working motherhood. Much of the world knows Huerta—correctly—as a tough negotiator, a strong leader. My image of her also includes Huerta the loving and devoted mother. And I don't think the two images conflict in the least.[42]

Chapter 3

Huerta, Cesar Chavez, and the NFWA

Dolores Huerta became even busier and more committed to her work during the next phase of her life, when she, together with another Community Service Organization leader, Cesar Chavez, cofounded the National Farm Workers Association (NFWA), a union dedicated to improving the working conditions for Mexican American farmworkers in the southwestern United States. The early years of this endeavor were difficult and full of sacrifice and struggle, but slowly the dedicated duo built up the membership of the union. Their dedication eventually paid off, as the union acquired nationwide prominence and began producing results in the form of increased wages and better working conditions for farm laborers.

The Agricultural Workers Association

Huerta first started organizing farmworkers on her own initiative when she was with the CSO. In 1958, together with a Catholic priest named Thomas McCullough, she founded a new organization within the CSO specifically directed at farmworkers—the Agricultural Workers Association (AWA). The goal of the group was to attract the interest and assistance of the

AFL-CIO, a powerful federation of labor unions in the United States created in 1955 through the merger of the American Federation of Labor (AFL) and the Congress of Industrial Organizations (CIO). The AFL-CIO had organized numerous factory workers throughout the country but had never tried to organize agricultural workers.

Huerta's work paid off. The following year, 1959, the AFL-CIO set up its own Agricultural Workers Organizing Committee (AWOC), and the AWA voted to merge into the AWOC. The AWOC then sent its own experienced union organizers to California to begin the drive to organize farm laborers. Over the next several years the organization poured more than $1 million into the effort.

Union organizers who had never done farmwork, however, had difficulty organizing poor migrant farmworkers who often lived in their cars or other transient places and were reluctant to

Union leaders meet at a 1950s AFL-CIO convention. Huerta got the labor organization to address the plight of farmworkers.

come to publicized union meetings. Instead of dealing directly with the workers, AWOC organizers tried to work with labor contractors who were paid by the growers to recruit, hire, and transport farm workers. These contractors often exploited farmworkers as much as their employers did. The AWOC also faced many other obstacles, including violations of the bracero program: Growers sometimes refused to hire available Mexican American residents in favor of more subservient Mexican nationals. Moreover, federal labor laws at that time did not protect the right of agricultural workers to picket and form unions.

In 1961 the AFL-CIO threatened to reduce funding for the farmworker project. Huerta became increasingly concerned that the AFL-CIO was not going to be successful in organizing California's farmworkers.

Huerta and Cesar Chavez

Despite the ongoing work of the AWOC, the real turning point for farmworker unionization came when Huerta started working with Cesar Chavez, the man who became her partner for the next thirty years. Like Huerta, Chavez had been recruited by Fred Ross years earlier to help set up a new chapter of the CSO. Chavez helped found the San Jose CSO and then worked with Ross to start a number of other chapters throughout California. Eventually Chavez moved up in the organization to become its national executive director.

Because of Ross's high regard for Chavez, Huerta expected him to be a dynamic, forceful person. When they first met at a fundraising dance in 1956, however, she instead saw someone who appeared shy and unassuming. Huerta recalls, "He was very quiet and humble. . . . He never fought for the limelight."[43] The two soon became close colleagues, both of them totally committed to improving the lives of farmworkers. Although they had two very different personalities, they shared one important trait—the inability to ignore the terrible injustices suffered by the poor migrant farmworkers who picked the produce on California's farms and vineyards. Many of these workers were Mexican Americans who spoke little English, and they were terribly exploited by farmers, often performing hard physical labor in the hot fields for hours on end, for extremely low wages, and without adequate water, food, or housing.

As time went on, both Huerta and Chavez became increasingly frustrated with the AFL-CIO's ineffective farmworker organization drive. Finally, in 1962, Chavez, then the CSO executive director, asked the organization's board of directors to support a separate CSO pilot project to organize farm laborers. At first the board agreed, but in March 1962 the idea was voted down at a CSO convention. Convention delegates wanted to focus the organization's resources on Chicanos who had left farmwork behind and were living in California's cities.

Following this defeat, at the end of the convention Chavez took a startling action: He abruptly resigned. Huerta explains: "[Cesar] dropped the bombshell on the convention. He had so much guts! Everybody was pressuring him to stay. People were crying. But he didn't bow to the pressure. He left."[44] Later Chavez told Huerta that he was going to start his own farmworkers union. "I was appalled," Huerta says, "the thought was so overwhelming. But when the initial shock wore off, I thought it was exciting."[45] Chavez officially quit the CSO on March 31, 1962, his thirty-fifth birthday, to begin what many saw as the almost impossible task of organizing a grassroots farmworkers union.

The Birth of the National Farm Workers Association

Chavez decided to begin preliminary union organization efforts in Delano, California, so he and his wife, Helen, and their eight children moved there. He chose Delano because his brother lived there and it was his wife's hometown; if times got hard, he believed his family would always be taken care of by extended family members and friends in the area. He soon called Huerta to help him with the union project. Huerta agreed immediately, even though she was then a single parent with many dependent children. Huerta remembers, "People thought I was a little loony because I was also going through a divorce and I had seven children and was going to quit my job . . . to come organize the union."[46] Because of her family obligations, however, Huerta continued working for the CSO in Stockton, spending many of her evenings and weekends driving to migrant labor camps in her old, battered car, with her children in tow, trying to interest farmworkers in the idea of a union. Soon Huerta decided to quit her job with the CSO and join Chavez in Delano. She says, "When I made the decision I was going to do

Cesar Chavez

Cesar Chavez was Dolores Huerta's partner and union soul mate for more than thirty years. Chavez was born on March 31, 1927, near Yuma, Arizona, the son of Mexican American parents. After his family was swindled out of their farm by dishonest whites, the family moved to California, settling near San Jose and doing farmwork. Chavez graduated from the eighth grade in 1942, but he then dropped out of school to earn money for the family as a migrant farmworker. He later educated himself by reading all kinds of books on subjects ranging from philosophy to economics. At age seventeen he enlisted in the U.S. Navy for two years. In 1948 he married Helen Fabela, with whom he raised a family of seven children. As an adult, Chavez became an organizer for the Community Service Organization, through which he met Huerta. Together, Chavez and Huerta dedicated their lives to the improvement of working conditions for farm laborers. In 1962 they cofounded the predecessor to the United Farm Workers, a union that eventually grew to nationwide prominence with Chavez as its main spokesperson. Chavez died peacefully in his sleep on April 23, 1993.

Cesar Chavez worked with Huerta for more than thirty years.

Despite the size and power of the AFL-CIO, shown here at its 1955 convention, Huerta and Chavez believed it did not do enough for farmworkers.

it, somebody left a big box of groceries on my front porch in Stockton, and I thought that was just like a sign to me."[47]

The strategy for building the union was to create it from the ground up, using simple grassroots organizing. First Huerta and Chavez chose the name National Farm Workers Association (NFWA) because they did not want to scare people who might be frightened by the idea of a union. Instead, they distributed NFWA survey cards simply asking workers for their names and addresses and what they thought was a fair wage. When people returned the cards, the organizers met with them to explain the NFWA's goals for improving working conditions.

The union was officially created at a founding convention, organized by Huerta and Chavez, on September 30, 1962, in Fresno. It was attended by about two hundred farmworkers. At the convention, Chavez and Huerta appeared onstage and described the NFWA's initial plans: to lobby the governor's office for a $1.50 per hour minimum wage for farmwork (workers then were receiving only $1.15 per hour) and unemployment insurance, to work for the right of farmworkers to unionize and engage in collective bargaining, and to establish a hiring hall and credit union for members. Chavez was elected president, and Huerta, along with two other friends of Chavez, Gil Padilla and Julio Hernandez, were elected vice presidents.

The fledgling NFWA adopted a bold Aztec eagle as its symbol, along with a slogan, *Viva La Causa*, meaning Long Live the Cause. The eagle design was chosen because it had straight lines and square corners that would be easy for people to reproduce. The colors chosen for the design were also simple: a white background for hope, a black eagle to symbolize the plight of the workers, and red lettering to represent the sacrifices that would soon be required.

Farmworkers pick and process celery on a California farm in 1959. Unionizing these workers increased their pay and benefits.

A Difficult Beginning

The NFWA convention was an exciting beginning, but afterward the hard work of developing the union began. Huerta and Chavez first took on the tasks of writing a constitution, finding a lawyer to do a legal incorporation, and lobbying in Sacramento. One of the most important early accomplishments, however, was the creation of a farmworkers' credit union. By mortgaging the house of Richard Chavez, Cesar's brother, the union was able to borrow money that it then loaned to workers. Many workers did not pay back their loans, and the union at first lost money on the endeavor, but the credit union gave farmworkers who could never have gotten help from commercial banks a service they desperately needed. As word spread about the credit union, the NFWA gained a reputation for helping the poor. The credit union went on to become a great success, eventually loaning more than $5.5 million to farmworkers.

FBI Surveillance of the NFWA

As Cesar Chavez, Dolores Huerta, and their union became more prominent, growers and other opponents openly began questioning their motivations. Some people accused them of being Communists who wanted to advance this political philosophy through their union efforts. Soon these comments attracted the interest of the Federal Bureau of Investigation (FBI), a U.S. government agency, which began spying on Chavez's and Huerta's activities. The FBI was particularly concerned about Huerta, especially after she gave an interview to *Peoples' World*, a Communist Party newspaper, in October 1965. The government became even more concerned when the union began attracting a wider following, including students and civil rights advocates who volunteered to help the farmworkers' unionizing efforts. The FBI surveillance lasted more than a decade and produced almost two thousand pages of documents for the agency's files. Eventually, however, the FBI determined that neither Chavez nor Huerta was affiliated with the Communist Party and neither had any intentions of threatening or undermining the U.S. government. The FBI concluded that they simply wanted to help improve the lives of farmworkers.

Another popular organizing tool for the NFWA was the publication of a farmworker newspaper, called *El Malcriado* (the child who talks back to his parents). The newspaper was funny and irreverent, with editorials that criticized low wages and unscrupulous farmers. It contained a cartoon of a hapless farmworker, Don Sotaco, a feature that helped to communicate the union's messages to farmworkers who could not read.

In the early days the union was almost flat broke and it struggled to survive. At the convention, it had been decided that the union would collect monthly dues of $3.50, but even that small amount of money was difficult for farmworkers to afford, and many did not pay it. Cesar, his wife, and his children earned a meager income by working in the fields, picking cotton and grapes. Huerta, too, barely survived, mostly on child support payments from her former husbands and a little unemployment insurance from her previous job. The financial hardships were difficult, but they were necessary to allow both Chavez and Huerta to devote all of their energies to building the union.

The NFWA's First Strike

In March 1965 the NFWA became embroiled in its first labor action. At this time in McFarland, a town near Delano, a number of farms grew roses, part of one of the biggest flower industries in the country. Workers on these farms had to graft rosebuds onto mature rosebushes—work that had to be performed with precision as well as great speed. At one of the farms, workers had been promised $9.00 for every thousand plants they grafted, but the farmer broke his word and instead paid them between $6.50 and $7.00 per thousand. One of the farmworkers from that company quit over the pay issue and came to Chavez and Huerta for help.

The NFWA organized meetings among the rose workers to discuss the situation, and the workers decided to strike the biggest rose company, Mount Arbor, for higher wages. Early on the first day of the strike, Huerta and other NFWA volunteers went to check on the workers, just to make sure they followed their promises not to report to work. When Huerta saw a group of workers awake and dressed, apparently ready to go to work, she

A French horticulturist grafts roses. The ill treatment of migrant workers who grafted roses in California inspired the 1965 farmworker strike.

drove her car into the driveway of the house where they were staying, blocking their car. Thanks to Huerta's vigilance and quick action, the strike went forward as planned.

The company responded at first by bringing in replacement workers from a small town in Mexico. After only three days, however, the rose company became desperate for its skilled workers to return. The company did not sign a contract with the union, but it agreed to a pay raise. News of the successful strike, which workers called the War of the Roses, spread throughout the region, enhancing the NFWA's growing reputation.

The Delano Grape Strike

Just months after the rose strike, in September 1965, the NFWA was reluctantly pulled into yet another labor action, one that soon made the union famous throughout the country. Trouble began when Filipino American farmworkers in nine vineyards near Delano went on strike for higher wages under the AFL-CIO's Agricultural Workers Organizing Committee (AWOC) banner. Workers at the vineyards became incensed when growers paid workers in another region $1.40 per hour but offered them only $1.00 per hour for the same work. The vineyard owners, however, brought in replacement workers, called scabs, and refused to honor the strike. After five days the growers also began shutting off electricity and gas to the striking workers' labor camps, located on company property. Tensions were rising

Migrant grape pickers vote to go on strike in 1966, an action that brought the farmworkers' union to the nation's attention.

Route of the First Delano March

Sacramento

Delano

CALIFORNIA

★ Sacramento

Lodi
Stockton
Manteca
Modesto
99 Turlock
Livingston
Merced
Chowchilla
99 Madera
Highway City
Fresno
Malaga
Parlier
Cutler
Visalia
Farmersville
Lindsay
99 Porterville
Ducor
65
Delano ☆

At a crucial point in the Grape Picker's Strike in 1966, Cesar Chavez and Dolores Huerta organized a 350-mile march from Delano to Sacramento, California. By the time Chavez reached Stockton, the group of protesters numbered 5,000. It was then that the first of the Delano growers contacted Chavez to sign a contract which guaranteed better pay and working conditions for the migrant laborers employed by the vineyards.

fast, with fights breaking out between strikers and scab workers. The AWOC asked the NFWA to support the strike to give it more legitimacy and help lift the spirits of the Filipino strikers.

Although the NFWA only had about twelve hundred members at this point—and only about two hundred who were paying dues—Chavez and Huerta decided it was time for all farmworkers to join the AWOC strike. They would have preferred to build the union for a few more years before embarking on such a difficult effort, but they saw it as an opportunity to expand the farmworker union movement beyond Delano to a much wider audience. Huerta immediately began working with the AWOC on their picket lines, and a meeting of the NFWA was scheduled for September 16, Mexican Independence Day, to see if their union members would go along with the idea.

When the day of the NFWA meeting arrived, the turnout was huge. Rumors about the strike had been building for days, and workers were ready for a fight. In the Delano area, grape pickers had long been frustrated by their wages—at that time they earned only about $2,400 a year, when the national definition of poverty was $3,223 per year for a family of four. The meeting ended with a vote for a general strike against all vineyards in the region, with wage demands the same as those of the AWOC. Workers also agreed that the strike would be nonviolent. Afterward Chavez and lawyers representing the NFWA tried to meet with the growers to negotiate, but the growers refused, fully expecting to be able to outlast the poor and desperate striking workers.

The more than two thousand workers who joined the strike, however, proved to be just as determined as their employers. Every morning they marched on picket lines at vineyards that spanned two counties. They shouted, "Huelga (strike)!"[48] and carried signs that conveyed the same message. They continued to picket as weeks and months ground by, even in the face of fierce grower intimidation. Some vineyard foremen, for example, drove equipment near the picket lines, covering picketers with dust. Other strike-breaking tactics included spraying the picket lines with pesticides, taunting the picketers with dogs, and calling them vicious names. Sometimes ranchers or their foremen even resorted to violence, stomping on picketers' toes, punching them in the ribs, or beating them up. Local police officers often ignored the violence and did not make arrests, showing their support for the growers. Huerta recalls, "It was like a war, a daily kind of confrontation. We never slept. We'd get up at 3:00 or 4:00 A.M. and then we'd go till 11:00 P.M."[49]

Despite these provocations, at the urging of Chavez, Huerta, and other strike leaders, the strikers remained nonviolent, resisting the urge to fight back. Huerta has credited having women on the picket lines as the key to this nonviolent strategy: "Women in the union are great on the picket line. More staying power, and we're nonviolent. One of the reasons our union is nonviolent is that we want our women and children involved, and we stay nonviolent because of the women and children."[50]

The Union

"Virtually all observers on the scene at that time [during the Delano grape strike] were convinced that, next to Chavez, Dolores Huerta . . . was the top leader of the union."

Sam Kushner, *Long Road to Delano*. New York: International, 1975, p. 157.

Chavez also has praised the role of women in the union, explaining, "The women are not afraid. They know what they're doing because it means beans and shoes for their kids."[51]

A National Stage

Although it was difficult and lengthy, the Delano grape strike quickly rocketed Chavez, Huerta, and the NFWA into the national limelight. Chavez began speaking before university and church groups, spreading word about the strike and asking for donations and support. Soon sympathizers started arriving in Delano and volunteering their help. Many were civil rights advocates, fresh from freedom marches that were then taking place in the southern United States, where African Americans and their supporters were protesting against segregation and racism. Newspapers and magazines also began publishing articles about the strike, and the publicity helped to fund and energize the farmworkers' strike movement.

One media highlight occurred in December 1965 when Walter Reuther, the president of the United Auto Workers (UAW), a large, well-respected industrial union, came to Delano to walk the farmworker picket lines. Afterward the UAW pledged five thousand dollars a month to both unions until the strike ended—a much-needed infusion of funds for the desperately poor NFWA. The union won another media victory in March 1966, when the U.S. Senate Subcommittee on Migratory Labor came to town to hold hearings on the strike. On the committee was Senator Robert Kennedy, who was symphathetic to labor. The hearing was covered by many reporters and it provided Chavez with a platform to speak about the police harassment of the strike and to lobby for the passage of laws to provide a higher minimum wage, prevent child labor, and provide collective bargaining rights to farm laborers. Before he left town, Kennedy, too, marched on the farmworker picket lines.

Even more publicity, however, came from a 300-mile (483 km) protest march from Delano to Sacramento that the union planned for March 17, 1966, to mark the six-month anniversary of the strike. Chavez and Huerta saw the march as a way to lift the sagging spirits of the strikers and bring attention to their plight. The march began with great excitement in Delano, with Chavez in the lead and about a hundred persons, mostly men, following. Huerta and most of the female union members stayed behind to keep the picket lines going. The marchers carried signs that read, "*Perigrin-*

acion, Penitencia, y Revolucion" ("Pilgrimage, Penitence, and Revolution"). Each night, they stopped to rest in towns along the way. Often at these designated stopping points, marchers found that residents had prepared huge feasts for them as a show of support for their cause. The protesters picked up new volunteers and marchers along the way, and soon the march had grown to include thousands of people.

Midway through the march, on March 25, 1966, Chavez was surprised by a message from the lawyer representing Schenley Industries, one of the companies targeted by the strike. Schenley, it turned out, was ready to settle with the union. A meeting was

National Farm Workers Association members try to persuade grape pickers to join their strike against growers in 1965.

quickly arranged, and the company agreed to recognize the NFWA as the bargaining representative for its farmworkers. Even though she had no experience negotiating labor contracts,

Bobby Kennedy and Huerta

As a legislative advocate for the United Farm Workers (UFW) for many years, Dolores Huerta met and befriended many politicians and led a number of campaigns to encourage Mexican Americans to register and vote in elections considered important for farmworkers. One of the most famous political friends of Huerta and the UFW was Robert "Bobby" Kennedy, the brother of the late president John F. Kennedy. In 1966 Senator Kennedy became a supporter of the farmworkers' union during the Delano grape strike. Two years later the union supported Kennedy when he ran for president in the 1968 Democratic primaries. On June 4, 1968, thanks in part to Huerta's political connections and efforts, Kennedy won the California primary. The following day Huerta was present onstage at a speech Kennedy gave to supporters in a ballroom of the Ambassador Hotel in Los Angeles. During the speech Kennedy thanked Huerta and Cesar Chavez for their help in registering large numbers of Chicanos to vote in the primary. Moments later, and just a few feet away from where Huerta was standing, Kennedy was shot and killed by an assassin.

Robert Kennedy (left) sits with Cesar Chavez in 1968.

Huerta was charged with handling the particulars of negotiating a full contract with the company. Years later Huerta explained how she did it:

> When Cesar put me in charge of negotiations in our first contract, I had never seen a contract before. I talked to labor people, I got copies of contracts and studied them for a week and a half, so I knew something when I came to the workers. Cesar almost fell over because I had my first contract all written and all the workers had voted on the proposals. He thought we ought to have an attorney, but really it was better to put the contracts in a simple language.[52]

As a result of Huerta's hard work, the two sides soon reached a final agreement that gave the workers a thirty-five-cent raise. It was the union's first labor contract—a sweet victory and one for which workers had paid a heavy price. As the Web site of the United Farm Workers, the successor of the NFWA, explains, "This was the first time in the history of the United States that a negotiating committee composed of farm workers negotiated a collective bargaining agreement with an agricultural corporation."[53]

The Firebrand

"Dolores was a 35 year old firebrand in 1965, and she was commanding crusty macho campesinos (Mexican peasants) 20 years her senior. . . . She led through persuasion and personal example, rather than intimidation, and . . . she was one hell of an organizer."

Luis Valdez, artist and writer. Quoted in Richard Griswold del Castillo and Richard A. Garcia, *Cesar Chavez: A Triumph of Spirit*. Norman: University of Oklahoma Press, p. 70.

After hearing of the contract, the joyful protesters marched on, reaching Sacramento on April 10, 1966. The large, exuberant crowd gathered on the steps of the capitol building, waving flags and wearing Mexican sombreros and colorful fiesta clothing. Dolores Huerta, sporting a cowboy hat and an ear-to-ear smile, was there to address the workers. She called on the state of

California to enact a collective bargaining law for farmworkers and warned, "You cannot close your eyes and your ears to us any longer. You cannot pretend that we do not exist. You cannot plead ignorance to our problems because we are here and we embody our needs for you. And we are not alone."[54] Chavez also spoke to the gathering, reminding them that "in victory there must be humility."[55]

It was a glorious day, but both Chavez and Huerta knew that one contract with a single grower was only the beginning for their new union. Numerous other growers were still resisting the farmworkers' strike, and much work remained for the NFWA.

Chapter 4

The Work of the UFW

With Cesar Chavez and Dolores Huerta leading the way, the NFWA—later called the United Farm Workers (UFW)—continued the Delano grape strike for five years. It was ultimately successful largely because of a nationwide consumer boycott that brought national attention to the plight of farmworkers. Indeed, during its heyday in the 1960s and 1970s, the UFW attracted a large membership, negotiated numerous labor contracts, and helped improve life for farmworkers in various other ways. Although Huerta often worked behind the scenes and allowed Chavez to act as the UFW's public spokesperson, the union's success was due in large part to her creative vision and the critical roles she played as organizer, negotiator, lobbyist, and strategist.

A Formidable Opponent

The 1965 Delano grape strike and the success of the contract with Schenley Industries catapulted the NFWA into a period of intense organizing within the grape industry. The next grape company to sign a contract with the NFWA was the DiGiorgio Fruit Corporation,

57

a huge agricultural company based in Arvin, California. It had more than 13,000 acres (5,261ha) of farmland in fruit production and over $230 million in annual sales. DiGiorgio also had a long history of trying to break unions and a reputation for using violence against strikers or anyone trying to unionize its workers. It agreed to work with the NFWA only after a fierce fight that sorely tested the new union and its leaders.

The battle with DiGiorgio began soon after the march on Sacramento. Chavez contacted the company to talk after the company representatives made public overtures on the radio suggesting it might be ready to negotiate. These initial negotiations were quickly called off by Chavez, however, after union members trying to talk with workers on one of DiGiorgio's ranches were

Striking grape workers picket against produce giant DiGiorgi in 1948.

threatened with violence. In response, the NFWA decided to hit DiGiorgio hard, using every weapon at the union's disposal. One of these weapons was a boycott of DiGiorgio's products, including its popular fruit juices and canned goods. During the boycott, strikers were sent to picket stores that sold these products in an effort to persuade consumers not to buy them. Picketers were also sent to the company's headquarters, shipping warehouses, and distribution centers around the country. The NFWA employed other tactics as well, such as convincing DiGiorgio's workers to strike from within by engaging in work slowdowns. This tactic involved various actions by workers to slow production and thereby cost the company money.

Making a "Sweetheart Deal"

The company countered the union's tactics with an unexpected but brilliant legal strategy—a plan to deliver its farmworkers to the International Brotherhood of Teamsters, a wealthy but corrupt union that was widely known to have ties to organized crime. The Teamsters were willing to make a "sweetheart deal" with the company—a deal that did not really protect the workers. By getting the Teamsters elected as the representative of the workers, DiGiorgio hoped to keep the NFWA away from its workforce. The struggle began when DiGiorgio suddenly announced in June 1967 that it would hold an election in just three days and allow its workers to choose among the NFWA, the AWOC, the Teamsters, or no union.

Faced with an immediate crisis, lawyers for the NFWA and the AWOC succeeded in getting a court to order that the two unions be removed from ballots before the election. Organizers also urged workers not to participate in what they viewed as an unfair union election. Despite these efforts, the company held the election and declared the Teamsters the winner. Still, the NFWA did not give up. Huerta lobbied the Mexican-American Political Association, an influential political group, to persuade California governor Edmund Brown to order a new election—a fair one that would be supervised by the impartial American Arbitration Association and held only after the NFWA had the chance to campaign for workers' votes. The stage was set for an epic confrontation. Journalists

Susan Ferriss and Ricardo Sandoval explain, "This was the upstart union's first election, and Chavez knew . . . if he didn't win, the NFWA might never recover."[56]

The Unheralded Heroine

"If Cesar Chavez is the hero of the Farmworkers movement, Dolores Huerta is its unheralded heroine. Huerta [played] a key organizing and leadership role."

Jean Murphy, writer. Quoted in Richard Griswold del Castillo and Richard A. Garcia, *Cesar Chavez: A Triumph of Spirit*. Norman: University of Oklahoma Press, p. 68.

To improve the union's strength and prepare for the election, the NFWA merged with the AFL-CIO's AWOC in July 1967 to become the United Farm Workers Organizing Committee (UFWOC), with Chavez as its leader. The new union then began around-the-clock organizing, trying to talk with every possible voter, often under the threat of Teamster violence. Organizers were even sent to Mexico to locate and return a group of migrant workers who had worked at DiGiorgio and were eligible to vote in the election. On the day of the election, the union gave voters rides to the polls.

The morning after the election, Huerta called from San Francisco, where the ballots were counted, announcing that the UFWOC had won the election among fieldworkers by 530 to 331 votes. It was an emotional victory for everyone. The union even received a congratulatory telegram from civil rights activist Martin Luther King Jr., who said, "As brothers in the fight for equality, I extend the hand of fellowship and good will. . . . You and your valiant fellow workers have demonstrated your commitment to righting grievous wrongs forced upon exploited people. We are together with you in spirit and in determination that our dreams for a better tomorrow will be realized."[57]

The fight with DiGiorgio was not over, however, because the election covered only two of its ranches. The UFWOC therefore immediately began work to unionize the company's third ranch in Arvin. As Huerta explains, this was a hard-fought battle: "DiGiorgio brought in a whole bunch of guys from Mexicali to vote against the Union. It's cheaper for them to bring in guys like that and pay them five hundred dollars apiece than it is to get a Union, in the long run."[58] Despite the challenges, the union won another election victory in November 1967 with 285 of 377 votes.

Following the elections Huerta was again put in charge of the contract negotiations—a difficult job that pitted her against trained, experienced company lawyers and negotiators who balked at even small workplace improvements. Nevertheless, the contract she negotiated with DiGiorgio established the first employer-paid health and welfare fund for farmworkers, provided for promotions and layoffs based on seniority, and gave workers vacation and holiday pay. After DiGiorgio signed a contract, some of the state's most well-known wineries, including Gallo, Christian Brothers, Almaden, and Paul Masson, also agreed to negotiate with the union. Huerta worked so hard on these nego-

Farmworkers' union members hoist Cesar Chavez onto their shoulders to celebrate his election victory over the Teamsters in 1966.

Huerta carries newspapers announcing the union-inspired boycott of table grapes in 1968.

tiations that she fainted from exhaustion and had to be admitted to the hospital for several days.

The National Grape Boycott

Despite its successes with DiGiorgio and other companies, the UFWOC still represented only a handful (about 5,000) of California's approximately 250,000 farmworkers. The Delano strike thus continued against many other grape growers. Chavez and Huerta chose Giumarra Vineyards, the state's biggest producer of grapes grown for eating, called table grapes, as the union's next target. "If we can crack Giumarra," Huerta reasoned at the time, "we can crack them all."[59] The struggle began in the fall of 1967, when the union held a large rally for Giumarra's workers. The workers voted to strike the company, and two-thirds of them—as many as eighteen hundred farmworkers—walked off the job in the middle of the grape harvest.

Giumarra fought back by hiring scab workers and sought court orders limiting picketing, and the strike dragged into the winter. It was then that Chavez and Huerta employed the union's most effective tool—a nationwide boycott of Giumarra. Huerta traveled to New York, the prime distribution site for grapes, along with some of her children and fifty farmworkers and volunteers, with plans to picket markets that sold grapes under any of Giumarra's six labels. Huerta had no idea how to do this, but she persevered. She later said, "There were no ground rules. I thought, 11 million people in New York, and I have to persuade them to stop buying grapes. Well, I didn't do it alone. When you need people, they come to you. You find a way."[60]

Giumarra fought the boycott by changing the labels on its grapes, a strategy that worked to confuse both consumers and picketers. To combat this, Huerta, together with her former Community Service Organization boss, Fred Ross, came up with the novel, and now legendary, idea of enlarging the Giumarra boycott to cover all nonunion table-grape growers in California. They convinced Chavez that this strategy would work, and union organizers were sent to distribution centers around the country to tell people to stop buying all nonunion grapes.

Without Fear

"Dolores is the only one I fight with, the only one who makes me lose my temper. I guess that's because I like her so much. That girl is something, really great. She's absolutely fearless, physically as well as psychologically."

Cesar Chavez. Quoted in M. Christie Mullikin and Carol Larson Jones, "Dolores Huerta: Cesar Chavez' Partner in Founding the United Farm Workers Union in California." www.csupomona.edu/~jis/1997/Mullikin.pdf.

Although it took several years, the boycott was a huge success. Journalists Ferriss and Sandoval state, "[The UFWOC's national grape boycott] became the most ambitious and successful boycott in American history."[61] It spread the union's message of fair working conditions nationwide, even among people who usually did not pay attention to social issues. Soon consumers across America stopped buying grapes, placing great public and economic pressure on the vineyards. Growers might be able to replace striking workers and continue production, but declining sales filled them with fear because low sales numbers directly and quickly affected company profits.

The shift toward widespread success in the table-grape industry began in mid-1969, when ten growers from Coachella, California, contacted the union asking to begin negotiations. In April 1970 Lionel Steinberg, who owned three of the biggest vineyards in Coachella, signed a contract with the union. Those who

A Florida family joins in the grape boycott by picketing outside a supermarket in 1969.

Chavez and other activists meet with grape grower John Giumarra Jr. (right) in 1970 to sign the contract ending the Delano grape strike.

settled with the union were able to market their grapes with a label showing the union eagle—a marketing tool that quickly brought them an influx of sales. Three months later, in July 1970, representatives from Giumarra Vineyards finally called Chavez, asking for a meeting.

The meeting was held at a motel in Delano; Huerta drove all night to get there. She and Chavez pushed for an industry-wide contract that would cover not only Giumarra but also the twenty-eight other growers that still had not agreed to negotiate with the union. After days of negotiations, Huerta succeeded in negotiating a historic three-year, industry-wide contract covering all twenty-nine growers. The contract, which was signed on July 29, 1970, provided for a hiring hall (a union-operated job placement center), an immediate pay increase from $1.65 per hour to $1.80

per hour, bonuses, pesticide protections, and employer contributions to an employee health and welfare fund. After a hard struggle, the union had won big. Huerta said at the time, "What's happened here is a miracle. . . . But it didn't come about by magic."[62] The vineyards were finally paying fair wages, and at this point the UFWOC had a growing membership of more than one hundred thousand workers.

Huerta's Role

The union's success was due in large part to Huerta's ingenuity, persuasiveness, intelligence, and toughness. From the start, she played the indispensable role of strategist and sounding board for Chavez, and she was instrumental in devising and then implementing the grape boycott plan. Her skills as a lobbyist, too, were often put to use, helping to gain political support for the union at key moments in its struggle against the grape growers. She also was a gifted organizer, helping to staff and maintain the union's picket lines throughout both the strike and the boycott.

In addition, Huerta excelled as the main negotiator of the union's initial contracts, somehow convincing obstinate growers to agree to conditions, such as pay raises, seniority provisions, and pesticide protections, that vastly improved the lives of farmworkers. Huerta explains:

> I think women are particularly good negotiators because we have a lot of patience, and no big ego trips to overcome. Women are more tenacious and that helps a great deal. It unnerves the growers to negotiate with us. . . . Growers can't swear back at us or at each other. And then we bring in the ethical questions, like how our kids live. How can the growers really argue against what should be done for human beings just to save money?[63]

Some grower representatives who faced Huerta across the negotiating table disliked her intensely and felt that she saw only her side in negotiations. Others, such as Arnold Myers, a California agricultural labor lawyer who negotiated with Huerta

Migrant workers pick lettuce on a California farm. A union-instigated national boycott of lettuce forced growers to improve treatment of workers.

over many years, considered her a tough and good opponent who always protected farmworkers' interests. He comments, "[Dolores Huerta] has very, very strong views about what she wants in contracts. . . . She's not afraid to say what she thinks."[64]

No Time to Rest

For Chavez and Huerta, there was no time to rest after their victory in the grape industry. Even before the Delano contract was signed, they were embroiled in yet another huge labor dispute. Just as DiGiorgio had tried to do, almost every major grower in California's Salinas Valley, a region then known as the world's largest producer of lettuce and other vegetables, signed sweetheart deals with the Teamsters. The growers took the action as a preemptive strike against the increasingly successful UFWOC, which they knew would soon make demands to represent their workers. Grower Daryl Arnold recalls, "The grape boycott scared the heck out of the farmers, all of us. . . . [The vegetable growers] thought if they could sign a contract with [the Teamsters] it would forestall Cesar [Chavez] trying to come in and take over the industry."[65]

The affected workers, numbering as many as eleven thousand, were given no choice over the matter and were fired if they refused to pay Teamster dues. Many were furious because they had been hoping to join the UFWOC. Chavez and Huerta decided that the UFWOC had to respond immediately or forever lose the chance to represent workers in the vegetable industry. The union soon put all its time and resources into organizing the vegetable workers, making legal challenges to the Teamsters' election, and pressuring California governor Ronald Reagan into calling for a fair election. The union also planned protest marches that, on August 2, 1970, brought more than three thousand farmworkers onto the streets and roads of Salinas Valley. Although workers were pressing for a strike, union leaders held back from such a step, because they needed more time to prepare. Behind the scenes, Chavez and Huerta were frantically planning both an industry-wide strike and another national boycott.

Strike Rumors

Rumors of an imminent UFWOC strike and boycott soon reached executives of the large agricultural companies that owned the Salinas Valley farms. Several growers sent representatives to meet secretly with the union, and Huerta and Chavez pushed them to persuade all the growers to break their Teamster contracts and hold a fair election. One large grower, InterHarvest, even agreed to negotiate with the UFWOC for a contract, after the union proved that it had collected union cards from 95 percent of the company's fieldworkers—a nearly unanimous showing of support. All efforts to work with other growers and avoid a strike failed, however, and at a rally on August 23, 1970, Huerta announced an industry-wide strike, reading a statement that said, "Everything we have done, we have done in good faith. Our good faith has been received with a slap in the face of farmworkers."[66]

The growers fought the strike with the usual methods: by hiring scabs and getting court orders against UFWOC picketing. Meanwhile, Teamster thugs with baseball bats used violence to try

Coretta Scott King, widow of Martin Luther King Jr., joins Chavez and others in a march to promote the lettuce boycott in New York City.

to keep UFWOC organizers, picketers, and protesters off growers' property. As in past farmworker strikes, the local police favored the growers and enforced the injunctions with their batons and guns drawn. With no end in sight, the UFWOC increased the pressure by declaring a boycott of all non-UFWOC lettuce. The boycott, too, was outlawed by a court injunction, and the union's challenge of the ruling caused Chavez to end up in jail.

Eventually the court rulings against the UFWOC were overturned on appeal, but the struggle with the Teamsters continued for years. Huerta, however, managed to win one surprising but key victory: She negotiated a generous contract with InterHarvest that granted its workers much more than the Teamster contracts, including large pay raises and a company promise to eliminate the use of DDT and other dangerous pesticides two years before the federal government acted to ban these substances. Weeks later several other growers rescinded their contracts with the Teamsters and also signed with the UFWOC.

As the strike continued, another positive development was the union's decision in 1972 to became an official member of the AFL-CIO, with full voting rights, changing its name to the United Farm Workers of America. Chavez became the UFW's president, and Huerta became its vice president. The change gave the UFW more control over its future, but it also required the union to be financially self-sufficient.

The Difficult Years

The next decade was a difficult one, during which the UFW lost contracts as well as members. The first sign of decline came in 1973, when the grape contracts negotiated in July 1970 expired and grape growers, like the vegetable growers in the Salinas Valley, signed sweetheart contracts with the Teamsters. It seemed that the UFW had barely begun learning how to administer its hard-won grape contracts when suddenly they were gone. The new Teamster contracts wiped out almost all of the earlier gains for farmworkers; workers returned to low wages and had no grievance procedures. Even worse, the contracts expired at a time when national politics did not favor the UFW; the country's president, Richard M. Nixon, had won the 1972 election with the support of the Teamsters, and he was prepared to do everything he could to assist the union and destroy the UFW. Despite these obstacles, in April 1973 more than a thousand grape workers went on strike to protest the Teamster takeover.

The next six months brought an orgy of Teamster violence against any farmworkers who dared display the UFW eagle symbol or in any other way show their support for the union. An all-too-familiar sequence of events unfolded, with courts issuing injunctions against UFW pickets and the police often ignoring blatant Teamster violence but using any excuse to arrest and jail UFW strikers. Altogether, more than thirty-five hundred farmworkers and their supporters were arrested, but most arrests were later thrown out by the courts. This strike soon became the most volatile and dangerous one in the union's history. Even the UFW's lawyer, Jerry Cohen, was brutally beaten by Teamster thugs, and two UFW members died on the union's picket lines. The struggle also sapped the union's finances.

Outraged by the violence, UFW leaders decided in the fall of 1973 to end the strike and stop the picketing until they could change the laws to protect the union's right to picket safely. In the meantime, the union focused on a nationwide boycott of nonunion lettuce and grapes. Huerta returned to the East Coast, where she led the boycott effort and organized broad support from feminists, community workers, religious groups, Hispanic associations, student protesters, and peace groups. This boycott, like the earlier grape boycott, was soon supported by millions of consumers, but growers continued to resist, and the Teamsters continued to gain more contracts.

The UFW began campaigning hard for a farm labor law that would guarantee workers the right to join a union of their choice. Federal labor laws such as the National Labor Relations Act guaranteed most workers the right to organize but did not cover the agricultural industry. No state law provided protection either. The

The NLRA and Farmworkers

Under the National Labor Relations Act (NLRA), legislation enacted by the U.S. Congress in 1935, the majority of U.S. workers employed by private companies are guaranteed the right to organize for purposes of bargaining collectively with their employer. Under the provisions of the law, if employees can show that they want to be represented by a particular union, for example by voting for union representation in an election, employers are obligated to bargain with them on pay and working conditions. The act also prohibits employers from firing workers engaged in union activities and gives employees the legal right to strike.

The NLRA, however, does not cover certain types of workers, such as agricultural workers, leaving them almost powerless, with no labor protections. As a result, growers historically have been able to block workers' efforts to form unions, conduct pickets and strikes, and force their employers to bargain with them. California's landmark Agricultural Labor Relations Act (ALRA), enacted in 1975, finally provided NLRA-type protections to California farmworkers. The ALRA does not completely solve the problems faced by farmworkers, though, because its effectiveness has long been hampered by inadequate state funding and weak enforcement.

UFW lobbied for California's new prolabor governor, Jerry Brown, to back the union's farm-labor proposal and push the state legislature to enact it.

Eventually Brown agreed to collaborate with the union on the issue. The UFW wanted a much stronger law, of course, than did the growers, and it specifically wanted the law to allow for UFW's most effective tool—its boycotts of all businesses that sold nonunion products, so-called secondary boycotts. Finally, on June 5, 1975, the union was able to claim victory with the passage of California's Agricultural Labor Relations Act (ALRA). The union accepted some compromises, but the new law met the UFW's main criteria: It protected the union's right to organize workers, provided for binding and secret-ballot union elections, allowed secondary boycotts under certain conditions, and required the appointment of the Agricultural Labor Relations Board (ALRB) to monitor compliance with the act's provisions and remedy unfair labor practices. To this day, the ALRA is the only labor law in the nation that protects agricultural workers.

After the new law was passed, the UFW renewed its drive to organize California's farmworkers, but the state's labor board often ruled against the UFW, limiting the union's ability to force fair elections. Nevertheless, after the first round of elections were finally held, the UFW had won at about 205 locations, covering about thirty thousand workers, while the Teamsters had managed to hold onto only 102 farms, covering about eleven thousand workers. More than two hundred thousand other farmworkers, however, were still unrepresented, so much more work and many challenges lay ahead for the UFW. But with a labor law and a group of solid contracts, Chavez and Huerta could finally feel confident that the union they had created would survive to continue the fight.

Chapter 5

The Fight Continues

After establishing itself as a permanent force in California agriculture in the 1960s and 1970s, the UFW continued to work tirelessly on behalf of farmworkers, fighting to enforce its contracts, winning new elections, and defending California's labor law against grower efforts to defund and weaken it. Through it all, Huerta stayed by Chavez's side, helping with boycott efforts and achieving a number of legislative victories for farmworkers, before finally stepping down from regular union work in the 1990s. Today, although Chavez has passed away, Huerta continues to fight for justice and equality, sometimes helping with UFW organizing efforts, speaking at various functions, and trying to encourage others to follow in her footsteps to become community organizers and activists.

The UFW Battles On

The passage of California's Agricultural Labor Relations Act was followed by many difficult years in which growers continued to work hand in hand with the Teamsters to constantly challenge the UFW's organizing efforts. Although the watchdog board set

Chavez signs autographs during a rally promoting Proposition 14 in 1976.

up by the legislation, the Agricultural Labor Relations Board, was awarded a $2.8 million budget for its first year, the board quickly ran out of money due to the large number of complaints filed. The lack of funding abruptly halted all enforcement efforts, and legislators refused to appropriate more money.

In response, the UFW turned to a new strategy—placing an initiative, Proposition 14, before the voters in the November 1976 California election. The proposition was designed to guarantee permanent funding for the ALRB and make the state labor law part of the state constitution to keep it from ever being repealed. In two months' time, the union quickly acquired seven hundred thousand signatures in support of the measure, more than enough to put the initiative on the ballot, and the threat that such a law might pass caused legislators to rapidly fund the ALRB. In the end, however, Proposition 14 was soundly defeated after growers sponsored a well-funded advertising campaign against it. It was one of the UFW's most crushing defeats.

Afterward the union went back to work trying to enforce its contracts under the less-than-perfect ALRA process and organizing more of the state's farmworkers. In 1976 the UFW won fifteen out of nineteen new elections, adding to its membership and list of contracts. A short time later even more good news came when the Teamsters union finally decided to withdraw from its representation of field farmworkers. In a private agreement, the two unions agreed that the Teamsters would retain one farmworker contract and otherwise focus on its representation of packinghouse and farm transportation workers, allowing the UFW to organize all remaining field farmworkers.

Thereafter, the UFW expected to win many new contracts. Yet instead, it faced another uphill labor battle when contracts with Salinas Valley vegetable growers expired at the beginning of 1979. The fight began when the union first met with growers to demand increases in wages and benefits in order to keep up with inflation and skyrocketing industry profits. The growers balked at the union's demands, leading quickly to what was called the great lettuce strike of 1979, in which more than five thousand workers left the fields and followed the harvest from farm to farm with pickets. Like past strikes, this one was hard fought and at times violent. This time, even many strikers abandoned the UFW's instructions to remain nonviolent, and at least one farmworker was killed when he was shot in the head by a ranch hand.

A Strong Foundation

"As difficult as [the UFW's] situation is now, and as hard as we have to fight now, we are blessed that Cesar and Dolores spent all of these decades building this foundation for us. That can't be replaced."

Arturo Rodriguez, UFW president. Quoted in Susan Ferriss and Ricardo Sandoval, *The Fight in the Fields.* New York: Harcourt Brace, 1997, p. 9.

The union was ultimately successful, however, in signing new contracts with most of the valley's vegetable farms. Thanks to the

UFW's efforts, entry-level wages for farmworkers at this point rose to over seven dollars per hour, and working conditions were significantly improved. Wages and conditions even improved at nonunion farms, merely because of the threat posed by the union's presence; farmers wanted to keep their workers happy so they would not be susceptible to UFW organizing efforts.

The UFW in Decline

During the 1980s and the 1990s, however, the UFW's fortunes declined substantially. Growers began letting UFW contracts expire and turned instead to labor contractors, who brought crews of desperate workers from Mexico who were willing to work cheaply and knew and cared little about unions. The union began winning fewer and fewer elections, and membership at one point dropped to only about twelve thousand active

Relatives of a farmworker killed in a violent confrontation between strikers and lettuce growers in 1979 mourn his loss.

Unionized air traffic controllers picket during their strike in 1981.

members. The union also faced long and expensive legal battles, trying to enforce its existing contracts against recalcitrant growers who challenged the union at every opportunity.

Many observers blamed the UFW leadership for this decline. Critics claimed the union had abandoned its grassroots organizing approach and that it was losing touch with farmworkers and focusing too much on big-city boycott activities. Others criticized Chavez for becoming too authoritarian, appointing only family members to positions of power, and destroying any chance for farmworkers to become UFW leaders through democratic elections. One former UFW organizer, Aristeo Zambrano, explains, "Chavez built the union and then he destroyed it. The U.F.W. self-destructed. When the Republicans came back in the 1980s and the growers moved against the union, there wasn't any farmworker movement left."[67]

Chavez, however, blamed the union's troubles on an ineffective state labor board and a shift in the political climate that supported

Thousands joined the funeral procession for Cesar Chavez, whose remains were carried in a simple pine coffin after his death in 1993.

grower-oriented policies and practices. After all, he pointed out, many other unions across the country were experiencing similar membership declines. Even the big industrial unions were in trouble due to cuts in manufacturing production, and politicians who once courted union votes became much less supportive of union ideas. President Ronald Reagan showed his contempt for unions during a massive air traffic controllers' strike in 1981 by firing all the strikers and replacing them with newly hired employees. By the end of the 1980s, only about 16 percent of all working Americans were represented by unions, a substantial drop since the beginning of the decade, when that number was 20 percent. This external antiunion climate and internal disagreements over the direction of the union, together with the UFW's long-standing policy of paying very low wages to its organizers, caused many longtime staff members to quit. Yet throughout it all, Huerta stayed with the UFW, loyal to Chavez.

To reinvigorate the union, in 1984 Chavez called for yet another grape boycott, this one focused on consumers' environmental concerns. For years the UFW had been increasingly worried about the danger of pesticide poisoning for farmworkers, so the environmental angle seemed perfect. In the 1980s, however, the

UFW lost significant ground as many of the companies signed by the union went out of business and those who remained turned to labor contractors for workers. Often, the workers were illegally brought in from Mexico and were therefore afraid to join the union. As a result, UFW membership fell from a high of around sixty thousand in the late 1970s to as few as five thousand in the early 1990s. During this period of struggle, Chavez unexpectedly died in his sleep on April 23, 1993, at age sixty-six. Many hoped his death would give new life to the union, as people were once again reminded of the UFW's original ideals and goals. Huerta expressed this hope in the eulogy she gave at Chavez's funeral, which was attended by more than thirty-five thousand people. "Cesar," she said, "died in peace, in good health, with a serene look on his face. It was as if he had chosen to die . . . at

Migrant workers plant squash on a farm. Most such workers today are undocumented and unconcerned about unionizing.

this Easter time. . . . He died so that we would wake up. He died so that the union might live."[68]

After Chavez's death his son-in-law, Arturo Rodriguez, became president of the union. With Huerta's help, over the years Rodriguez has tried to rebuild the UFW by initiating a new wave of organizing and signing numerous new contracts with growers. Rodriguez's victories include the UFW's first agreement in twenty-seven years with the Gallo winery as well as contracts that protect about 70 percent of mushroom workers on California's central coast and about 50 percent of Central Valley rose workers. Another of the industries targeted by Rodriguez was California's

Dolores Huerta waits to be introduced at one of her many speaking engagements.

$800 million strawberry industry. In March 2001 the UFW finally won its first big victory in this latest organizing battle, signing a contract with Coastal Berry, the nation's largest strawberry grower. The contract provided for significant wage increases and generous benefits that included free health care, a dental plan, a seniority system, six paid holidays, a vacation plan, and job guarantees. Rodriguez explained at the time, "It gives the union a major stake in the strawberry industry."[69]

Today California is the producer of more than half the vegetables and fruits consumed in the United States, and virtually all of this produce is still picked by hand by farmworkers, many of whom continue to work for low pay under terrible conditions. The UFW's struggle for farmworkers thus continues.

Huerta's Later Achievements

During the years before Chavez's death, Huerta focused largely on politics, legislative lobbying, and public speaking duties. As head of the union's political arm, the Citizens' Participation Day Department, during the 1970s and the 1980s she kept up a frantic pace—speaking at countless labor and other events, raising funds, and promoting UFW boycotts. She explains, "My duties are policy-making like [those of] Cesar Chavez. It is the creative part of the organization. I am in charge of political and legislative activity. Much of my work is public relations."[70]

During this period Huerta also testified passionately before Congress on a number of issues important to farmworkers, and she helped win the passage of several important pieces of legislation. In 1974, for example, she helped to secure legislation that required unemployment benefits to be paid to laid-off farmworkers. In 1975 she lobbied against federal guest-worker programs and pushed for legislation to grant amnesty to Mexicans who had traveled to the United States illegally but who had lived, worked, and paid taxes in the United States for many years. Amnesty ultimately was granted to such workers in the Immigration Act of 1985, benefiting about nine hundred thousand farmworkers.

In addition, Huerta became involved with the union's efforts to protect workers from dangerous pesticides such as DDT, parathion, and methyl bromide. The use of pesticides has been shown to have significant effects on workers' health, including increasing risks for cancer and serious birth defects in babies whose parents come into contact with the chemicals. The lack of adequate health insurance for farmworkers only increases the threat of these dangers. Many of the early agreements that Huerta negotiated for the union contained clauses prohibiting the use of pesticides. She later lobbied for laws to ban various pesticides and promote better field protections for workers.

Another important project of Huerta's was Radio Campesina, a radio station founded by the union with the call letters KUFW. The station was a tremendous help to the UFW's organizing efforts because it enabled the union to reach the farmworkers' community easily and quickly. Radio Campesina still exists today, broadcasting to about 450,000 Latinos living throughout California.

A Close Call

In 1988, at age fifty-eight, Huerta was still as active as ever, involved with various UFW activities, when an unexpected event brought her work to an abrupt stop. In September of that year Huerta was severely injured when she was beaten by baton-wielding police officers at a protest rally. The beating occurred outside the Sir Francis Drake Hotel on Union Square in San Francisco, where Huerta was participating in a peaceful demonstration against the pesticide policies of vice president and presidential candidate George H.W. Bush, the father of current president George W. Bush. Huerta was standing at the front of the crowd when it surged forward, pressing her against the police barricade. She was trying to move back, as instructed by the police, when a policeman drove his riot baton into her body.

Huerta survived the beating but sustained serious injuries, including multiple broken ribs and a ruptured spleen (an organ important to the body's immune system). She was rushed to the hospital for emergency surgery, and along the way she lost so much blood that she could have died. Doctors had to completely remove her spleen. She was released after an extended hospital stay, but full recovery took months. Fortunately, for her the brutal assault was filmed by a local television station. In 1991 that video evidence helped Huerta sue the city of San Francisco and negotiate a record out-of-court settlement of $825,000. At the time Huerta joked that now she would finally have to open a checking

Huerta and Chavez

Dolores Huerta spent more than thirty years working with Cesar Chavez. Although they were cofounders of the United Farm Workers, Chavez became the visible public leader for the union, and Huerta became the person who implemented union policy and decisions, often outside of public view. Over the years the two leaders became extremely close, almost like brother and sister, and stayed in constant contact.

Their relationship, however, was sometimes difficult; both were stubborn and opinionated and had very different personalities. Whereas Chavez was quiet, calm, and determined, Huerta was fiery, outspoken, and combative. According to reports, these differences often led to bitter fights. Huerta herself has stated, "Cesar and I have a lot of personal fights, usually over strategy or personalities. I don't think Cesar himself understands why he fights with me." Despite their disagreements, Chavez and Huerta always maintained great respect and affection for each other. In addition to her considerable organizing, negotiating, and lobbying skills, Huerta provided Chavez with honest advice and unfailing loyalty throughout his life.

Quoted in Richard Griswold del Castillo and Richard A. Garcia, *Cesar Chavez: A Triumph of Spirit*. Norman: University of Oklahoma Press, p. 60.

Huerta and Chavez strategize under photos of Robert Kennedy and Mohandas Gandhi.

account. Later, the money became Huerta's only retirement fund. Huerta's lawsuit was also successful in getting the city's police department to change its crowd-control procedures to limit the use of batons and potentially dangerous police tactics during protests.

Following this life-threatening scare, Huerta took a break from union activities. She had often found herself in dangerous positions during her long UFW career, and she had been arrested more than twenty times, but she had never been convicted. This was the first time, however, that she became the victim of violence. She took a leave of absence from the UFW to recover her health and to work on women's issues.

Huerta the Feminist

Between 1991 and 1993 Huerta traveled around the country speaking on sexual harassment issues and lobbying against federal and state legislation that negatively affected women. Two of the laws Huerta opposed, however, were eventually enacted: the Welfare Reform Act, a federal law passed in 1996 that limits welfare benefits and gives states more control over their distribution, and California's 1996 Proposition 209, which prohibits preferential treatment based on race, gender, color, ethnicity, or national origin in state employment, education, and contracting, thereby denying members of many minority groups the benefits of affirmative action programs. Huerta also spent much of this period encouraging Latinas to run for public office as part of a campaign called the Feminist Majority's Feminization of Power.

Huerta wanted to do this work because she felt that she had not done enough for women earlier. She explained to *Ms.* magazine in 1998, "In the sixties and seventies, many of us were working hard to get justice for la raza [ethnic Mexicans], not for women. We should have been doing more for women at the same time. We've had to do a lot of catching up."[71] Many admirers of Huerta, however, believed she led other women through example, and her many successes in a male-dominated union and culture had already done much to advance the rights of women.

Huerta has often talked about the sexism she faced and how she tried to deal with it. "For a long time I was the only woman on the [UFW] executive board," she recalls, "and the men would

Dolores Huerta (center) joins a march in 2006 to celebrate Cesar Chavez's birthday and to protest proposed anti-immigrant legislation.

come out and say their stupid little jokes about women. So I started keeping a record. At the end of the meeting, I'd say, 'During the course of this meeting you men have made 58 sexist remarks.' Pretty soon I got them down to 25, then ten, and then five."[72]

Just before he died, Cesar Chavez acknowledged that he had treated Huerta differently from other UFW workers. Huerta comments, "And I said, 'Yes, Cesar, it's male chauvinism.' He laughed and laughed . . . [but] that was his indirect way of apologizing to me."[73]

Today, despite her long dedication to the UFW, her close partnership with Chavez, and her many achievements, Huerta is still given only scant recognition in most of the books and articles that have been written about the UFW. As *Ms.* magazine reporter Julie Felner puts it:

> Perhaps the greatest irony of Huerta's career is that you're more likely to find a detailed report of her activities in FBI files and police records than in the pages of history books. . . . While volumes have been devoted to Chavez's life, a search through the library

for articles about Huerta yields little more than a smattering in progressive magazines. Much of why Huerta was never given her proper due is pure and simple sexism.[74]

Later Years

Following Chavez's death in 1993, Huerta returned to the UFW to help it transition to a new generation of leaders. In the role of a wise elder statesperson and secretary-treasurer of the UFW executive board, she toured the country speaking on behalf of the union to a wide variety of labor, women's, political, and community groups. In the late 1990s Huerta threw herself into more UFW organizing campaigns, once again heading up the union's collective-bargaining department. Her organizing effort in the strawberry industry focused on what Huerta called "a motherhood campaign,"[75] which sought living wages, job security, clean drinking water and toilets in the fields, decent housing, health care, a medical plan, and the freedom to work without sexual harassment. In her late sixties, Huerta could be found leading marches and speaking at forums throughout the country to publicize the campaign.

In 1999 Huerta resigned from her position as secretary-treasurer of the UFW's executive board to campaign for Al Gore in the 2000 presidential race. In the fall of 2000, however, she was hospitalized several times when a near-fatal condition put her health in great jeopardy. She had surgery to repair problems related to a rare opening of the aortic artery in her intestines, and she remained in critical condition for several weeks. Later she was stricken with pneumonia. Always a fighter, she urged supporters to vote for Gore from her hospital bed. After convalescing for several months, surrounded by her large family, she regained her health and resumed her appearances and speaking engagements at a slightly slower pace.

Since then Huerta has continued to speak out about issues important to women and Mexican Americans. Now in her seventies, she still travels around the country to educate people about public policy issues affecting farmworkers, immigrants, and women. In the summer of 2002 she even led a 165-mile (266km)

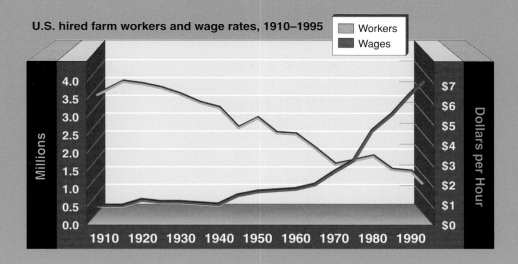

Dolores Huerta's Contribution to Fair Wages

U.S. hired farm workers and wage rates, 1910–1995

Workers
Wages

Millions

Dollars per Hour

march to Sacramento in 100 degree (37°C) heat in support of a state bill to give farmworkers increased bargaining power. In September 2003 California governor Gray Davis appointed her to serve on the University of California Board of Regents. That same year Huerta launched the Dolores Huerta Foundation, a private entity that hopes to train a new generation of community activists. In 2004 she toured the country as chair of the National Women's Campaign on behalf of the presidential campaign of Senator John Kerry. In 2006 Huerta spoke out to praise the tens of thousands of Latinos who staged protests in several U.S. cities against proposed legislation that would criminalize illegal immigration and penalize anyone who hires illegal immigrants or provides them with assistance. "Thank goodness the people are rising up and saying this is not right,"[76] she says.

Huerta's Legacy

Today Huerta's life is an inspiration to all people who seek social justice and equality. For more than fifty years Huerta has dedicated herself to improving the lives of farmworkers, some of the poorest and least powerful people in the United States, and to fighting for fairness in society for all people. As Luis Valdez, a Mexican American artist who worked with Huerta often over the years, once commented, "The wonder of Dolores Huerta is that she has never given up struggling for what's right, decent

Arturo Rodriguez

Arturo Rodriguez was chosen to lead the United Farm Workers (UFW) after Cesar Chavez's death in 1993. Rodriguez was born on June 23, 1949, on a small farm outside San Antonio, Texas, the son of a sheet metal worker and a schoolteacher. As a young man Rodriguez attended Catholic schools in San Antonio, graduating in 1967 from high school and then earning a bachelor of arts degree in sociology at St. Mary's University in 1971 and a master's degree in social work from the University of Michigan in 1973. Rodriguez first became active in the UFW in 1969 as a college student. He later worked on boycott campaigns in Detroit, organizing drives in California, and various other political activities. He married Chavez's daughter, Linda, in 1974, and they have had three children. In 1981 Rodriguez was elected to the UFW's executive board, and for years he worked closely with Cesar Chavez on a number of projects, taking on increasingly more responsibility. As president, he has implemented major organizing drives that have resulted in the UFW winning twenty-one union elections and signing twenty-five new contracts.

Arturo Rodriguez and Dolores Huerta lead a march in 2002.

and human in the world, and she never will."[77] Her unwavering commitment to her vision, her great strength, intelligence, political savvy, and her wide-open heart have made a strong impression on many people and have won her many friends. She has felt equally at home talking with poor Mexican farmworkers as she has working and socializing with influential American leaders such as presidential candidate Robert Kennedy, civil rights leader Coretta Scott King, and feminist Gloria Steinem.

Champion for Civil Rights

"Dolores Huerta has always stood up for the oppressed. Her courage and leadership was crucial in the long fight to establish the United Farm Workers and to bring humane working conditions and basic rights to migrant farm workers. She has always been a champion of civil rights."

Edward M. Kennedy. Quoted in Bonnie Dahl, "Mission Dolores," *Prism Online*, October 1995. www.journalism.sfsu.edu/www/pubs/prism/oct95/mission.html.

Huerta's remarkable character traits and her peaceful political advocacy have also won her multiple awards. In 1984, for example, the California Senate recognized her with the Outstanding Labor Leader Award. In 1993 she was inducted into the National Women's Hall of Fame and received several awards, including the American Civil Liberties Union's Roger Baldwin Medal of Liberty, the Eugene V. Debs Foundation's Outstanding American Award, and the Ellis Island Medal of Freedom. In 1998 she was selected to be one of three of *Ms.* magazine's "Women of the Year" and one of the *Ladies' Home Journal's* "100 Most Important Women of the 20th Century." That same year President Bill Clinton awarded her the U.S. Presidential Eleanor D. Roosevelt Human Rights Award. In 2002 she received the James Smithson Award from the Smithsonian Institution as well as the prestigious Nation/Puffin Award for Creative Citizenship, an honor that was accompanied by a one-hundred-thousand-dollar prize. She also has been awarded honorary doctorate degrees from several universities and has served on government commissions as well as the boards of the Fund for the Feminist Majority and numerous other political and civil rights groups.

Huerta poses with President Bill Clinton in 1999 after receiving the Eleanor Roosevelt Human Rights Award.

Huerta's own words best describe her true purpose and lasting legacy. When asked about the UFW's greatest contribution, she replied, "I think we brought to the world, the United States anyway, the whole idea of boycotting as a nonviolent tactic. I think we showed the world that nonviolence can work to make social change."[78] She also has said, "I would like to be remembered as a woman who cares for fellow humans. We must use our lives to make the world a better place to live, not just to acquire things. That is what we are put on earth for."[79] Another time, when asked what she wanted on her tombstone, Huerta answered simply by stating the unofficial motto of Chavez and the UFW—"Si se puede [It can be done]!"[80]

Notes

Introduction: A Passion for Justice

1. Quoted in Bonnie Dahl, "Mission Dolores," *Prism Online*, October 1995. www.journalism.sfsu.edu/www/pubs/prism/oct95/mission.html.
2. Quoted in *La Voz de Aztlan*, "Viva La Causa," March 27, 2000, vol. 1, iss. 7. www.aztlan.net/default7.htm.
3. Quoted in M. Christie Mullikin and Carol Larson Jones, "Dolores Huerta: Cesar Chavez' Partner in Founding the United Farm Workers Union in California." www.csupomona.edu/~jis/1997/Mullikin.pdf.

Chapter 1: Lessons from Childhood

4. Quoted in Margaret Rose, "Dolores Huerta: Labor Leader, Social Activist," in *Notable Hispanic American Women*, ed. Diane Telgen and Jim Kemp. Detroit: Gale, 1993, p. 211.
5. Quoted in Margaret Rose, "Dolores Huerta: Passionate Defender of La Causa." http://chavez.cde.ca.gov/ModelCurriculum/Teachers/Lessons/Resources/Documents/Dolores_Huerta_Essay.pdf.
6. Quoted in Susan Ferriss and Ricardo Sandoval, *The Fight in the Fields*. New York: Harcourt Brace, 1997, p. 61.
7. Quoted in Frances Ortega, "Interview with Dolores Huerta," Voices of the Earth, Southwest Research and Information Center, October 29, 2003. www.sric.org/voices /2004/v5n2/huerta.html.
8. Quoted in Mullikin and Jones, "Dolores Huerta."
9. Quoted in Julie Felner, "Woman of the Year: Dolores Huerta," *Ms.*, January/February 1998.
10. Quoted in Richard Griswold del Castillo and Richard A. Garcia, *Cesar Chavez: A Triumph of Spirit*. Norman: University of Oklahoma Press, pp. 62–63.
11. Quoted in Griswold del Castillo and Garcia, *Cesar Chavez*, p. 64.

12. Quoted in Griswold del Castillo and Garcia, *Cesar Chavez*, p. 64.
13. Quoted in Dahl, "Mission Dolores."
14. Quoted in *Teaching to Change LA*, "Interview with Dolores Huerta, Community Leader and Activist," vol. 4, no. 1–3, 2003–2004. www.tcla.gseis.ucla.edu/equalterms/dialogue/2/huerta.html.
15. Quoted in Dahl, "Mission Dolores."
16. Quoted in Griswold del Castillo and Garcia, *Cesar Chavez*, p. 65.
17. Quoted in Dahl, "Mission Dolores."
18. Quoted in Griswold del Castillo and Garcia, *Cesar Chavez*, p. 66.
19. Quoted in *Teaching to Change LA*, "Interview with Dolores Huerta, Community Leader and Activist."

Chapter Two: Mother and Social Activist
20. Quoted in Griswold del Castillo and Garcia, *Cesar Chavez*, p. 66.
21. Quoted in Dolores Huerta Foundation, "Dolores Huerta Biography," www.doloreshuerta.org/dolores_huerta_foundation.htm.
22. *La Voz de Aztlan*, "Viva La Causa."
23. Quoted in Jacques E. Levy, *Cesar Chavez: Autobiography of La Causa*. New York: W.W. Norton, 1975, p. 95.
24. Quoted in Griswold del Castillo and Garcia, *Cesar Chavez*, p. 65.
25. Quoted in Ferriss and Sandoval, *The Fight in the Fields*, p. 61.
26. Quoted in Barbara L. Baer and Glenna Matthews, "You Find a Way: The Women of the Boycott," *Nation*, February 23, 1974.
27. Quoted in Dolores Huerta Foundation, "Dolores Huerta Biography."
28. Quoted in Griswold del Castillo and Garcia, *Cesar Chavez*, p. 68.
29. Quoted in Levy, *Cesar Chavez*, p. 146.
30. Quoted in Dahl, "Mission Dolores."
31. Quoted in Dahl, "Mission Dolores."
32. Quoted in Dahl, "Mission Dolores."

33. Quoted in Griswold del Castillo and Garcia, *Cesar Chavez*, p. 60.
34. Quoted in Felner, "Woman of the Year."
35. Quoted in Dahl, "Mission Dolores."
36. Quoted in Baer and Matthews, "You Find a Way."
37. Quoted in Felner, "Woman of the Year."
38. Quoted in Felner, "Woman of the Year."
39. Quoted in Baer and Matthews, "You Find a Way."
40. Quoted in Ortega, "Interview with Dolores Huerta."
41. Quoted in Vicki Ruiz, "From out of the Shadows: Mexican Women in the United States," *Organization of American Historians Magazine of History*, Winter 1996, p. 10. www.oah.org/pubs/magazine/latinos/ruiz.html.
42. Jone Johnson Lewis, "Women's History: Dolores Huerta," 1999–2006. http://womenshistory.about.com/library/bio/blhuerta.htm.

Chapter Three: Huerta, Cesar Chavez, and the NFWA
43. Quoted in Levy, *Cesar Chavez*, p. 146.
44. Quoted in Levy, *Cesar Chavez*, p. 147.
45. Quoted in Levy, *Cesar Chavez*, p. 147.
46. Quoted in Ferriss and Sandoval, *The Fight in the Fields*, p. 77.
47. Quoted in Ferriss and Sandoval, *The Fight in the Fields*, p. 77.
48. Susan Ferriss and Ricardo Sandoval, *The Fight in the Fields*, New York: Harcourt Brace, 1997, p. 101.
49. Quoted in Mullikin and Jones, "Dolores Huerta."
50. Quoted in Baer and Matthews, "You Find a Way."
51. Quoted in Levy, *Cesar Chavez*.
52. Quoted in Baer and Matthews. "You Find a Way."
53. United Farm Workers, "Dolores Huerta Biography." www.ufw.org/dh.htm.
54. Quoted in Ferriss and Sandoval, *The Fight in the Fields*, p. 122.
55. Quoted in Ferriss and Sandoval, *The Fight in the Fields*, p. 123.

Chapter Four: The Work of the UFW
56. Ferriss and Sandoval, *The Fight in the Fields*, p. 131.
57. Quoted in Levy, *Cesar Chavez*, p. 246.

58. Quoted in Levy, *Cesar Chavez*, p. 253.
59. Quoted in Dick Meister and Ann Loftis, *A Long Time Coming.* New York: MacMillan, 1977, p. 151.
60. Quoted in Mullikin and Jones, "Dolores Huerta."
61. Ferriss and Sandoval, *The Fight in the Fields*, p. 139.
62. Quoted in Meister and Loftis, *A Long Time Coming*, p. 164.
63. Quoted in Baer and Matthews, "You Find a Way."
64. Quoted in Dahl, "Mission Dolores."
65. Quoted in Ferriss and Sandoval, *The Fight in the Fields*, p. 161.
66. Quoted in Ferriss and Sandoval, *The Fight in the Fields*, p. 170.

Chapter Five: The Fight Continues
67. Quoted in Frank Bardacke, "Cesar's Ghost: Decline and Fall of the U.F.W.," *Nation*, July 26, 1993. www.thenation.com/doc/19930726/bardacket/6.
68. Quoted in Bardacke, "Cesar's Ghost."
69. Quoted in Eric Brazil, "UFW, Strawberry Grower Sign Historic Labor Contract," *San Francisco Chronicle*, March 9, 2001. http://apmp.berkeley.edu/APMP/alra/ctnrepts/contract30901.html.
70. Quoted in Griswold del Castillo and Garcia, *Cesar Chavez*, p. 69.
71. Quoted in Felner, "Woman of the Year."
72. Quoted in Felner, "Woman of the Year."
73. Quoted in Dahl, "Mission Dolores."
74. Quoted in Felner, "Woman of the Year."
75. Quoted in Pat Broderick, "Fearless Organizer Fights for Strawberry Workers," *San Diego Business Journal*, April 7, 1997, vol. 18, no. 14, p. 31.
76. Quoted in Louie Gilot, "Activist Urges Fighting Immigration Reform," *El Paso (TX) Times*, March 25, 1006. www.elpasotimes.com/apps/pbcs.dll/article?AID=/20060325/NEWS/60324005/1001.
77. Quoted in Griswold del Castillo and Garcia, *Cesar Chavez*, p. 70.
78. Quoted in *La Voz de Aztlan*, "Viva La Causa."
79. Quoted in Griswold del Castillo and Garcia, *Cesar Chavez*, p. 71.
80. Quoted in Dahl, "Mission Dolores."

Important Dates

April 10, 1930
Dolores Clara Fernandez is born in Dawson, New Mexico, to Juan and Alicia Fernandez.

1933
Huerta's parents divorce.

1936
Huerta's mother moves the family to Stockton, California.

1947
Huerta graduates from Stockton High School.

1948
Huerta marries Ralph Head; the marriage eventually ends in divorce.

1955
Huerta graduates from the University of the Pacific; she begins working for the Community Service Organization (CSO); she meets and marries Ventura Huerta.

1956
Huerta meets Cesar Chavez, who also works for the CSO.

1958
Huerta helps found the Agricultural Workers Association.

1961
Huerta separates from Ventura Huerta.

March 1962
Chavez resigns from the CSO, and he and Huerta dedicate themselves to organizing farmworkers.

September 30, 1962
The National Farm Workers Association (NFWA) is officially founded, with Chavez as president and Huerta as vice president.

95

1962–1965
Chavez and Huerta work to increase the membership of the union.

March 1965
The NFWA organizes rose workers and calls for its first strike.

September 1965
The NFWA votes to join a strike against Delano-area grape growers begun by the Agricultural Workers Organizing Committee (AWOC), beginning the five-year Delano grape strike.

March 1966
The NFWA stages a march from Delano to Sacramento, and Huerta negotiates the union's first contract with Schenley Industries.

Spring–Summer 1966
The NFWA orders a boycott of the DiGiorgio Fruit Corporation, forces it to hold an election, and wins the election; Huerta negotiates the contract.

July 1967
The NFWA and the AWOC merge to form the United Farm Workers Organizing Committee (UFWOC).

Fall 1967
The UFWOC stages strikes against Giumarra Vineyards, an effort that expands into a nationwide grape boycott.

1968
Huerta travels to New York to promote the boycott.

April 1970
Vineyard owner Lionel Steinberg signs a contract with the UFWOC.

July 29, 1970
Giumarra Vineyards and twenty-eight other grape growers sign a contract with the UFWOC.

1970
Huerta begins a long-term relationship with Richard Chavez, Cesar Chavez's brother.

Summer 1970
All the major vegetable growers in California's Salinas Valley sign contracts with the Teamsters, and the UFWOC announces an industry-wide strike.

1972
The UFWOC becomes the United Farm Workers of America (UFW).

1973
The UFW's grape contracts expire, but growers sign contracts with the Teamsters, sparking a UFW strike and a second grape boycott.

June 5, 1975
The UFW successfully lobbies the California legislature to pass the Agricultural Labor Relations Act (ALRA), a law to protect the bargaining rights of farmworkers.

1975–1976
Hundreds of elections are held and the UFW wins the majority of those in which it participates, but the Agricultural Labor Relations Board (ALRB) runs out of money, disrupting enforcement of the ALRA.

1976
The UFW loses in its drive to enact Proposition 14, which would have provided permanent funding to the ALRB.

1977
The Teamsters agree to withdraw from organizing field farmworkers, leaving the UFW free to organize those workers.

1979
The UFW contracts with vegetable growers expire, leading to a strike and boycott, followed by a UFW contract with most of the growers.

1980s
The UFW loses many of its contracts, and membership declines, but Huerta works on legislative matters and wins several victories.

1986
The UFW begins another grape boycott to draw public attention to the pesticide poisoning of farmworkers.

September 1988
Huerta is beaten and severely injured by police at a demonstration in San Francisco.

1991–1993
Huerta takes a leave of absence from the UFW to work on women's issues.

April 23, 1993
Cesar Chavez dies peacefully in his sleep.

May 1993
Arturo Rodriguez, Chavez's son-in-law, becomes union president; Huerta returns to the UFW to help ease the transition.

1994–2000
The UFW begins a new organizing drive and signs many new agreements with growers.

1999
Huerta resigns from the UFW to campaign for Al Gore in the 2000 presidential race.

Fall 2000
Huerta is hospitalized with a near-fatal health condition.

2002
Huerta leads a march to Sacramento in support of a state bill to give farmworkers increased bargaining power.

2003
California governor Gray Davis appoints Huerta to serve on the University of California Board of Regents.

2006
Huerta speaks out in support of immigration protests.

For More Information

Books

John Gregory Dunne, *Delano: The Story of the California Grape Strike*. New York: Farrar, Straus & Giroux, 1967. Although it contains almost no references to Dolores Huerta, this is a detailed history of the UFW's first grape strike and boycott.

Sam Kushner, *Long Road to Delano*. New York: International, 1975. A well-written history of the early days of the UFW.

Peter Mathieson, *Sal Si Puedes: Cesar Chavez and the New American Revolution*. New York: Random House, 1969. A dated but useful biography of Cesar Chavez and the farm worker unionization movement.

Rebecca Thatcher Murcia, *Dolores Huerta*. Bear, DE: Mitchell Lane, 2003. A relatively up-to-date biography of Huerta, written for children.

Frank Perez, *Dolores Huerta*. Austin: Steck-Vaughn, 1996. A biography of Huerta written for children.

Catharine de Ruiz and Richard Larios, *La Causa: The Migrant Farmworkers' Story*. Austin: Steck-Vaughn, 1993. A history of the UFW, including the work of Chavez and Huerta, written for children.

Web Sites

Dolores Huerta Foundation (www.doloreshuerta.org/index. htm). A Web site for Huerta's nonprofit organization, which works to teach community organizing techniques to new leaders.

The Fight in the Fields (www.pbs.org/itvs/fightfields/ resources.html#Anchor-Cesar). A Web site that focuses on a 1997 Public Broadcasting System documentary about Cesar Chavez and the UFW and provides narrative information about the film, Chavez's life, and the history of the UFW.

United Farm Workers (www.ufw.org). A Web site run by the UFW that provides information about the union's history as well as its current activities.

Walter P. Reuther Library (www.reuther.wayne.edu/ufw-article.html). A Web site run by Wayne State University that contains a narrative history of the UFW as well as a listing of union materials contained in the university's collection.

Index

101

Picture Credits

About the Author

Debra A. Miller is a writer and lawyer with a passion for current events and history. She began her law career in Washington, D.C., where she worked on legislative, policy, and legal matters in government, public interest, and private law firm positions. She now lives with her husband in Encinitas, California. She has written and edited numerous books and anthologies on historical and political topics.